IMAGES
of America

GREENE COUNTY
AND MESOPOTAMIA
CEMETERY

ON THE COVER: In the late 1850s, Capt. Edwin Reese (1812–1891), a prominent Greene County carriage manufacturer, built the Greek Revival mansion Basil Hall. One of four surviving pillared mansions in Eutaw, it is listed on the National Register of Historic Places and still stands, complete with Reese family portraits. Edwin was a descendant of David Reese, signer of the famous Mecklenburg Declaration of Independence in Charlotte, North Carolina, in 1775, and the son of Henry Dobson Reese and Rebecca Harris of Pendleton, South Carolina. Edwin and his wife, Charlotte McKinstry, both buried in Mesopotamia Cemetery, were the parents of nine children, seven of whom lived to adulthood. Edwin was a Civil War captain of the home guard, which organized as Captain Reese's Militia in Eutaw. His son Carlos, also buried in Mesopotamia, served as a Confederate army private in Fowler's/Phelan's Battery Artillery. (Library of Congress, Prints and Photographs Division, HABS-ALA, 32-EUTA, 4-2.)

IMAGES
of America

GREENE COUNTY AND MESOPOTAMIA CEMETERY

Kimberly R. Jacobson and
the Greene County Historical Society

ARCADIA
PUBLISHING

Published by Arcadia Publishing
Charleston SC, Chicago IL, Portsmouth NH, San Francisco CA

Library of Congress Catalog Card Number: 2007928190

For all general information contact Arcadia Publishing at:
Telephone 843-853-2070
Fax 843-853-0044
E-mail sales@arcadiapublishing.com
For customer service and orders:
Toll-Free 1-888-313-2665

Visit us on the Internet at www.arcadiapublishing.com

CONFEDERATE MONUMENT. The Confederate monument, with its south-facing soldier, stands in the front of Mesopotamia Cemetery. It was unveiled on April 24, 1908, by the Ladies Memorial Association of Greene County, a group that later organized as the Greene County chapter of the United Daughters of the Confederacy. Erected in memory of the Confederate dead, the monument is inscribed with the surnames of 387 Greene County soldiers.

CONTENTS

ACKNOWLEDGMENTS

Many thanks to everyone who helped make this book possible. I first thank my husband, Tom Jacobson, for his patience, enthusiasm, and encouragement. Secondly, my sister Cheryl Schmenk for her companionship, chauffeuring, and research assistance during our annual genealogy-related forays that first sparked my interest in Greene County. Thanks are extended to my niece Heather Griffin, a student at the University of Alabama, for her insight and assistance. Some of the many Greene County descendants who provided material and photographs include Ann Banks, Betty C. Banks and her staff at the *Greene County Independent*, Teresa Beeker, the Blantons, Susan Bookless, Alice Campbell, Carole Phillips, and Jack Winston.

Eutaw local Sue Vance, particularly helpful in pointing me to the area's best resources, deserves special thanks for the over-500 holiday luminaries that she arranges in Mesopotamia Cemetery each December. I am grateful to the Greene County Historical Society for preserving the architecture of the era, providing many of the photographs and background material used in this book, and showing its overall support for the project. Unless otherwise noted, all photographs are courtesy of the Jacobson collection.

Finally, posthumous thanks go to V. Gayle Snedecor (my hero) for his effort to publish an indispensable map and directory of the Greene County area in the 1850s. The background provided by Mary Morgan Glass in her book *A Goodly Heritage: Memories of Greene County* was indispensable, as was Clay Lancaster's *Eutaw: The Builders and Architecture of an Antebellum Southern Town*.

INTRODUCTION

Originally known as Oak Hill Cemetery, Mesopotamia Cemetery was established around 1822 on present-day Mesopotamia Street in Eutaw, Alabama. Local planter Alexander Shaw deeded the property to the trustees of the church in 1833 for the sum of $1 to "build a church and academy." The Mesopotamia Presbyterian Church, serving the Scotch-Irish planters of the area, was one of the earliest in Greene County. It was disassembled after the congregation migrated to the First Presbyterian Church in Eutaw. Located behind the original church, the still-active cemetery is currently maintained by the City of Eutaw.

The first regular minister of the Mesopotamia Presbyterian Church was Rev. John Hannah Gray (1826–1836), the South Carolinian husband of Charleston heiress Jane Robertson. Gray was a man of spiritual as well as intellectual attainments and began instructing slaves to become members in full communion with the church. Gray followed a policy laid down by the Presbyterian Church in 1787 stating that slaves ought to "be given such good education as to prepare them for the better enjoyment of freedom," with a goal of bringing about "the final abolition of slavery in America." This ministry to slaves in Eutaw was continued after Gray resigned in 1836.

Reverend Gray and his brother-in-law Robert G. Quarles are credited with naming Greene County after Revolutionary War hero Gen. Nathaniel Greene and Eutaw after the Revolutionary War Battle of Eutaw Springs. Quarles surveyed and laid out the town lots of Eutaw in 1838 on 20 acres conveyed by Asa White, an early settler and local plantation owner. The village of Mesopotamia slowly disappeared as the nearby city of Eutaw became the county's commercial and residential hub. Greene had become the most populous county in the state of Alabama by 1850 and was widely regarded for its thriving and elegant communities. Rivers on three of its four borders provided ample transportation for the crops grown in the primarily agricultural county. The Golden Age of Greene County lasted from 1840 until the Reconstruction era after the Civil War.

Greene County is part of Alabama's Black Belt, a term first used to describe the dark, fertile soil. The area was perfect for agriculture and therefore a popular area for plantation owners to relocate with their slaves. After the Civil War, the term became primarily political, to describe counties in which the African American population outnumbered the white population. Per the 2000 census, Greene's population is 80 percent African American, with 40 percent of the county below poverty levels.

The area is rich in cultural traditions and the strength of its people. Distinguished burials in Mesopotamia Cemetery include state senators Solomon McAlpine, Joseph W. Taylor, and James Daniel Webb and state representatives James Blair Clark, Richard Freer Inge, William Bacon Oliver, and John J. Winston. Military notables include Confederate war hero Col. Stephen Fowler Hale, a member of the Alabama legislature for whom Hale County was named; Maj. Gen. Daniel H. Byrd, commander of the 12th Division of the Georgia Militia during the Mexican War; and Col. Joseph Pickens, the youngest son of Gen. Andrew Pickens, for whom Pickens County was named.

Merchants of note include John DuBois, a manufacturer of cotton gins who earned three patents on improvements made to the DuBois Cotton Gin. Collectors of Southern coin silver will recognize the mark "G. Braune" inscribed on the backside of their now-rare silver spoons. Jeweler and silversmith Gustave Braune and his family are buried in Mesopotamia, and Braune's home on Prairie Street in Eutaw is still occupied by descendants.

Eutaw Marble Works supplied many of the tombstones in Mesopotamia from the 1840s until the late 1870s. White marble was the primary material used for headstones due to its abundance in Alabama after the discovery of marble in the Sylacauga area of Talladega County. Mesopotamia Cemetery boasts a variety of tombstone styles rich in symbolism and well-versed epitaphs signed by well-known Alabama carvers.

This book focuses on Eutaw and Greene County's beginnings by sharing with the reader a pictorial overview of some of the earliest settlers now buried in Mesopotamia Cemetery. Portraits, documents, photographs of residents' homes, businesses, and final resting places serve to chronicle the rich history of this quaint, antebellum Southern town.

COL. ASA WHITE RESIDENCE. The home of Col. Asa White (1783–1861), located on Mesopotamia Street in Eutaw, looks virtually the same as it did when it was built in the 1830s. White, one of the earliest settlers of Greene County, conveyed a 20-acre square to the City of Eutaw in 1838 to be used for the courthouse, civic buildings, and commercial district. The White Home, per Clay Lancaster's *Eutaw: The Builders and Architecture of a Southern Antebellum Town*, is said to have "set the standard for the more pretentious homes of Eutaw" and is now on the National Register of Historic Places. Colonel White and his wife, Rebecca (1801–1876), were both interred in Mesopotamia Cemetery. (Library of Congress, Prints and Photographs Division, HABS-ALA, 32-EUTA, 11-1.)

One

EARLY ARRIVALS

Rev. Andrew Brown (1764–1823), organizing pastor of the Mesopotamia Presbyterian Church, followed his congregation to Alabama after serving the Bethel Church in South Carolina. Brown had been the first pastor of Bethel Church, having helped organize their ministry in 1805.

Many of the earliest arrivals in the Mesopotamia vicinity and burials in the Mesopotamia Cemetery were members of the Mesopotamia Presbyterian Church's first congregation. This small group of Presbyterians, organized by the Tuscaloosa Presbytery in 1824, included James Dunlap and his wife, Mary; William C. Baskins and his wife, Margaret; Philmon Buford and his wife; Sarah Brown, the widow of Rev. Andrew Brown; Mrs. Neal; Mrs. McDow; and Ben and Becia Buford, the slaves of Philmon Buford. In 1824, the ruling elders consisted of William C. Baskins, Alexander T. Shaw, Abner A. Steele, and James Hall Archibald.

Alexander Shaw and his wife, Susan, deeded property to the trustees of the Mesopotamia Church (William M. Lewis, James Rives, Arthur Slaughter, James Hall Archibald, and John Creswell) for "the building of a Church and Academy" in 1833. A male academy was built on the land and conducted by the Presbyterians. The Mesopotamia Presbyterian Church was erected and then later disassembled after the congregation migrated to the Eutaw Presbyterian Church in 1851.

The earliest date of death inscribed on an extant tombstone is that of Alexander Steele (1795–1828), the son of Abner Alexander Steele and Elizabeth Deale. The Steeles traveled to the Mesopotamia area from South Carolina before Alabama became a state in 1820. Abner was one of the first officers of the church, and his sons William, Elihu, and Robert served as ruling elders.

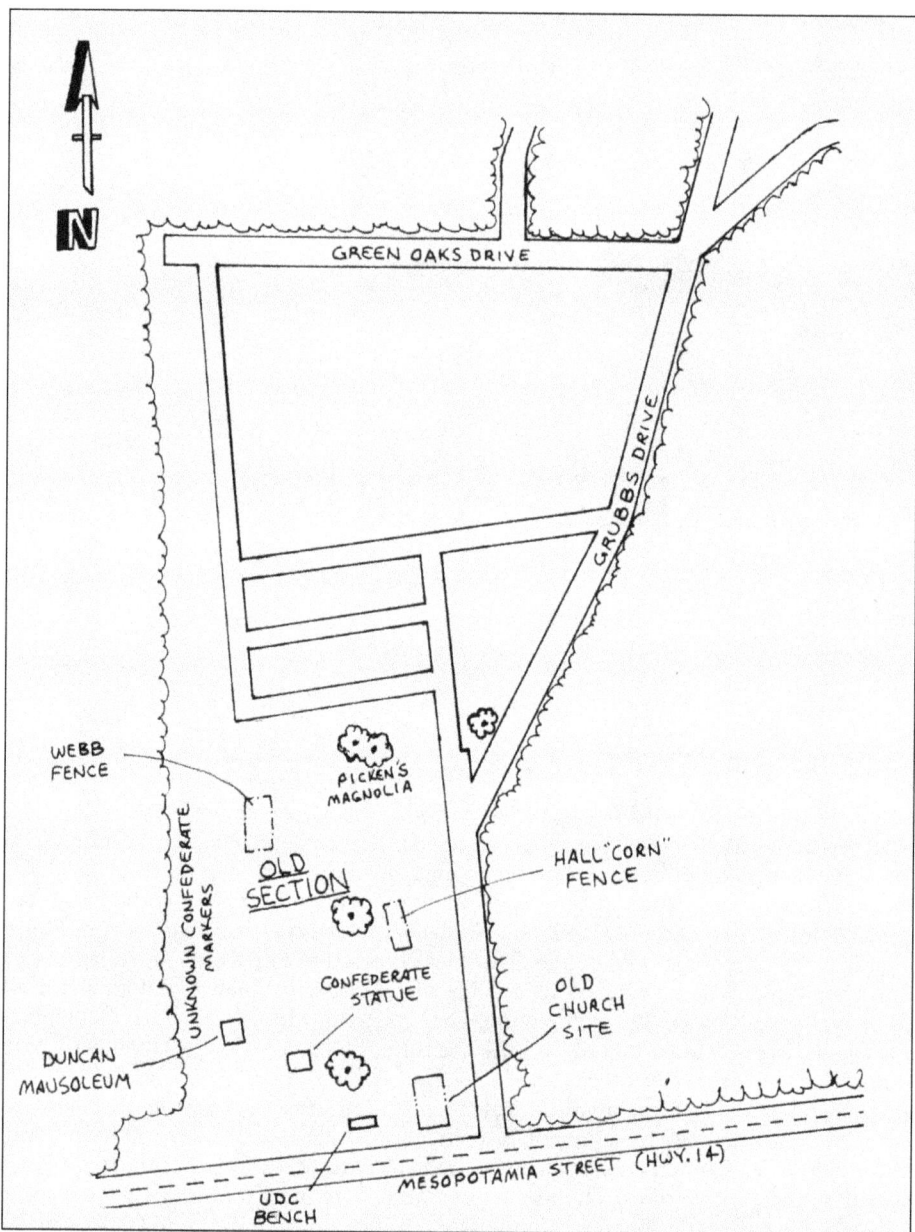

OVERVIEW MAP OF MESOPOTAMIA CEMETERY. Mesopotamia Cemetery is located on Mesopotamia Street (Highway 14) in Eutaw, about two miles east of Interstate 20/59 at the Eutaw exit. The oldest section of the cemetery is closest to Mesopotamia Street, though descendants of the old lines are still being buried near their kin. The cemetery is maintained by the City of Eutaw, in whose office are blueprints containing lot sales. In the early 1900s, the Ladies Memorial Association (now defunct) erected a gate with a sign for the cemetery that no longer exists. In a June 1855 article entitled "That Grave-Yard from the Eutaw Whig and Public Advertiser," a call was made to the citizens of Greene County "for some steps to have been taken for its repair and proper arrangement" so that "the grave would lose much of its cheerless gloom, and be more like the quiet resting place of sleeping friends." Unfortunately, the call is relevant again today, as many old marble stones are broken and sadly laying in a state of disrepair.

EUTAW PRESBYTERIAN CHURCH, INTERIOR. The Mesopotamia Presbyterian Church (1824–c. 1851), which once stood on the cemetery property, served the Scotch-Irish planters of the area as one of the earliest churches in Greene County. The church was disassembled after the congregation migrated to the Eutaw Presbyterian Church in 1851. (Library of Congress, Prints and Photographs Division, HABS-ALA, 32-EUTA, 10-6.)

REV. JOHN HANNAH GRAY. The first regular pastor of the Mesopotamia Presbyterian Church, Rev. John Hannah Gray was a pupil of Moses Waddel at his distinguished academy in Willington, South Carolina. He served as pastor from 1826 to 1836, before becoming the president of LaGrange College in Georgia from 1857 to 1862. (Second Presbyterian Church, Memphis, Tennessee.)

11

EBENEZER PRESBYTERIAN CHURCH, C. 1890. James Dunlap (1759–1844), one of the earliest settlers of the Mesopotamia area, and his wife, Mary (see page 21), were the parents of nine children. Their son John Baskin Dunlap lived in the Clinton precinct of Greene County and attended the Ebenezer Presbyterian Church. (Clinton Cross.)

BETH SALEM PRESBYTERIAN CHURCH, BOLIGEE, BUILT C. 1840. Nicholson Ross Morgan (1789–1881), the son of Enoch and Jane (Ross) Morgan, served as interim pastor at Mesopotamia in 1839 and at numerous other small churches in the area, including Pleasant Ridge Presbyterian Church and Beth Salem Presbyterian Church. (Library of Congress, Prints and Photographs Division, HABS-ALA, 32-BOLI, 1-1.)

Rev. David Davidson Sanderson (1821–1891). Reverend Sanderson was one of the area's longest-term pastors, serving from 1860 to 1891. The congregations of the New Hope Presbyterian Church and the Eutaw Presbyterian Church erected a monument in his honor in Mesopotamia Cemetery inscribed as follows: "Our Beloved Pastor: Rev. D. D. Sanderson. Erected by the congregation of Eutaw and New Hope Churches. David Davidson Sanderson Nov. 15, 1821 May 15, 1891."

Abner Alexander Steele (1768–1842). Abner A. Steele, the son of Aaron Steele and Violet Alexander, married Elizabeth Deale, the daughter of Clement Deale of Pendleton District, South Carolina. Abner and his brother Aaron were among the earliest arrivals in Greene County. Abner and Elizabeth, both buried in Mesopotamia, were the parents of 13 children.

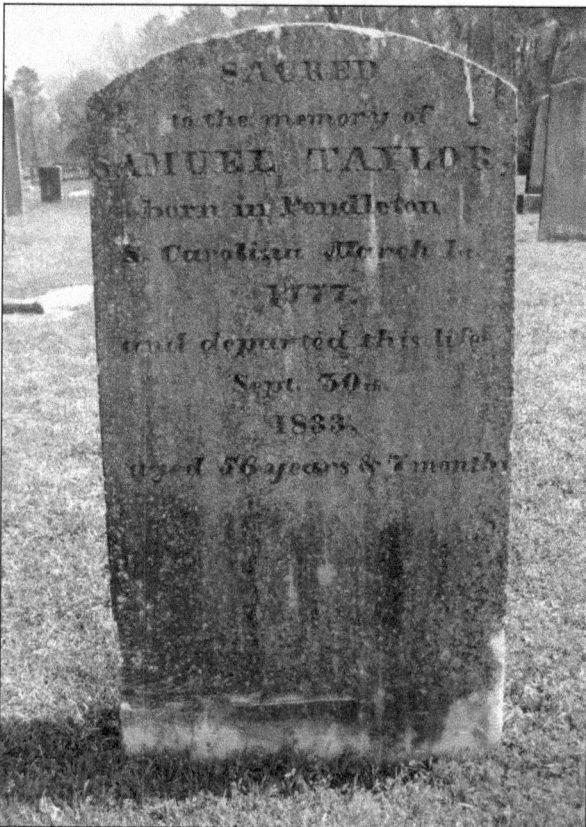

PLEASANT RIDGE PRESBYTERIAN CHURCH AND CEMETERY. William Steele (1807–1859), the son of Alexander and Elizabeth Steele, moved to Pleasant Ridge in Greene County and became one of the charter members and first ruling elders of the Pleasant Ridge Presbyterian Church. William married Eleanor Kennedy, the daughter of Thomas Kennedy and Elizabeth Potter.

MAJ. SAMUEL TAYLOR (1777–1833). Maj. Samuel Taylor of Pendleton District, South Carolina, was the son of Maj. Samuel Taylor of Revolutionary War fame. The younger Taylor was one of the first burials in Mesopotamia. According to the *Genealogy of the Reese Family in Wales and America,* "He and his son-in-law, Mr. Bacon, were the last men to drive the Indians out of Greene County into the Sipsey Bottom." The tombstone is signed "G. Herd, Eutaw."

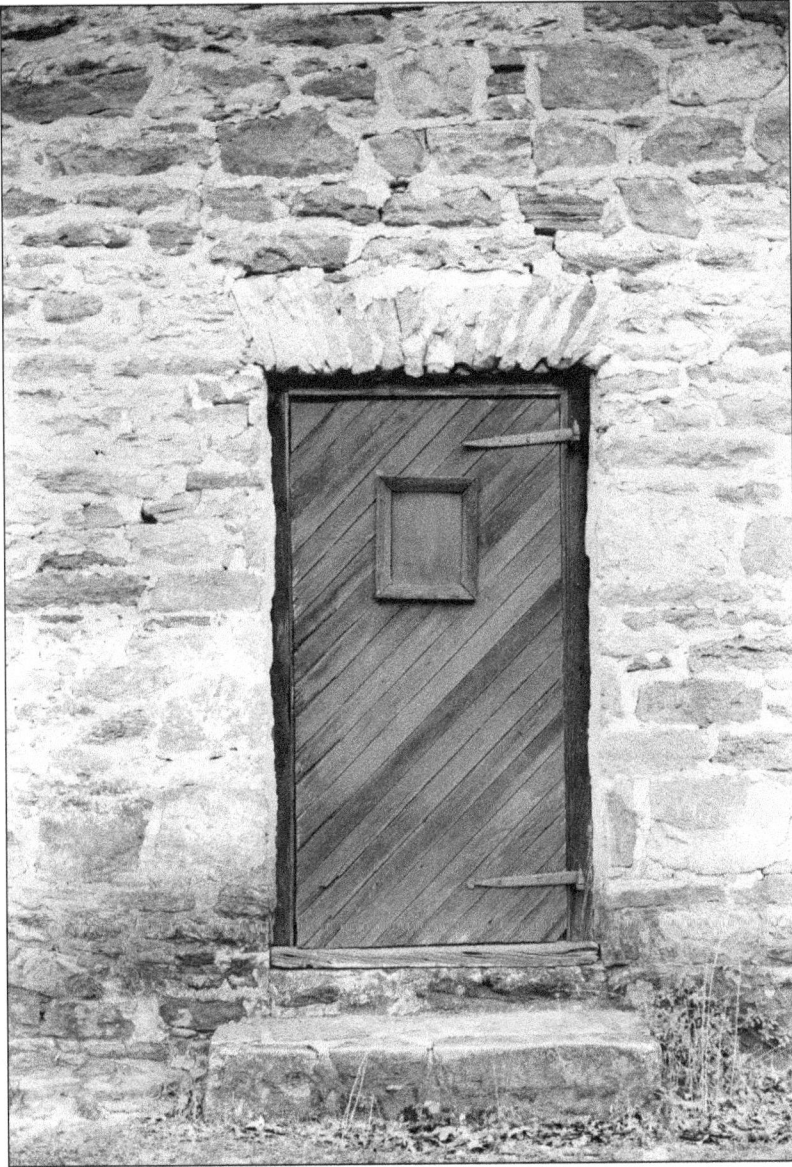

HOPEWELL MEETING HOUSE, SOUTH CAROLINA. Maj. Samuel Taylor's wife, Leah Reese (1779–1836), was the eldest daughter of patriot Rev. Thomas Reese (1742–1796), the first pastor of the Hopewell Meeting House, also known as the "Old Stone Church," in the Clemson vicinity of present-day Oconee County. The church was built between 1797 and 1802 by John Rusk and is now listed on the National Register of Historic Places. Rusk, a stonemason who immigrated to South Carolina from Ireland in 1791, is buried in the cemetery with his wife, Mary Sterritt. Their son Thomas Jefferson Rusk was very influential in Texas history, contributing significantly to the drafting of the state constitution. He was the first Secretary of War of the Republic of Texas and served as a state senator from 1846 to 1857. Many Greene Countians descended from those buried in the church's cemetery, including Gen. Andrew Pickens and his wife, Rebecca, who donated the pulpit and seats for the church. The home on the cover of this book belongs to Leah Reese's nephew Edwin Reese. (Library of Congress, Prints and Photographs Division, HABS-ALA, 37-CLEM.V, 1-2.)

EARLY BURIALS, JUDITH AND JUBAL HILL. Jubal O. N. Hill, who died in 1835, is buried next to his mother, Judith Hill (1811–1836). The wife of J. W. Hill, she died at the age of 25. The style of the Hill tombstones is consistent with early marble carver Edward Gantt, though neither stone is signed.

JAMES M. RICHARDSON (1836–1838). Early Mesopotamia residents laid to rest James Richardson, the infant son of Drusilla and Grief Richardson. Drusilla was the daughter of Samuel and Leah (Reese) Taylor. According to the *Genealogy of the Reese Family in Wales and America*, Grief Richardson of Virginia is said to have received his name because "his father died shortly before his birth, and his mother, being so crushed with sorrow and trouble, at his birth called him Grief; but he proved the joy of her old age."

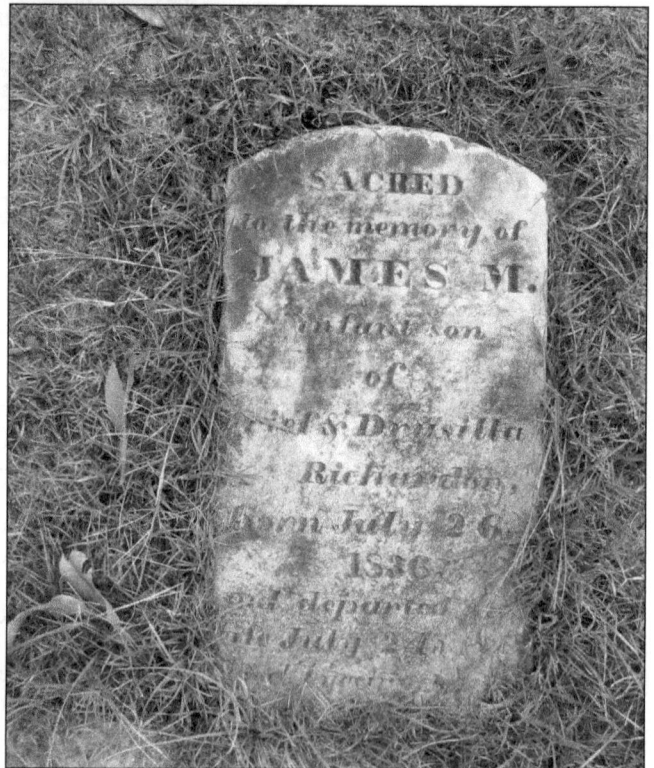

ELIZABETH SHEA (1775–1834). Shea's marble headstone is in remarkably fine shape, considering that it has withstood the Alabama sun for almost 175 years. The monument displays willows and urns, common symbols of mourning after the Revolutionary War. The column on the left of the willow represents a noble life, and the drapery above the inscription represents sorrow and mourning.

ANGELINA PARK (D. 1839). The marble tombstone of Angelina Park, the wife of Dr. A. T. Park and the daughter of Dr. James and Mrs. L. C. Meacham, is also well preserved. The iconography on the top of Angelina's gothic-style headstone depicts one of the more literal funerary symbols. The three stages of this insect's life—caterpillar, chrysalis, and butterfly—are easily recognizable as symbols of life, death, and resurrection.

FREDERICK FOSTER (1775–1838).
Frederick Foster was born in Andover,
Massachusetts, in 1775, the son of Obadiah
Foster and Hannah Ballard. He married
Nancy Finch of Newberry District, South
Carolina, and died in Mesopotamia at
the age of 63. The cross moline carved on
Frederick's headstone is one of the oldest
heraldic variations of the cross.

**FOSTER-HERNDON HOME, MESOPOTAMIA
STREET.** In 1836, Frederick Foster built
a home that was originally attached
to this two-story house west of the
cemetery. Nancy Foster, who sold it to
Emma S. Herndon (see page 99) in 1843,
died in 1857 and is buried next to her
husband in Mesopotamia Cemetery. The
structure is now known as the Herndon-
Liverman home. (Greene County
Historical Society.)

Two

MESOPOTAMIA MARBLE CARVERS

Early Mesopotamia tombstones were purchased from a wide variety of talented carvers, with white marble being the most popular material for 19th-century burials. Marble was imported from Italy and Vermont, as well as the Sylacauga Marble Belt in Talladega County. Dr. Edward Gantt, a surgeon under General Jackson, is credited with being the first to discover marble on his Sylacauga farm in 1820.

The Herd brothers of Perth Shire, Scotland, first quarried marble in the vicinity of Dr. Gantt's discovery before purchasing their own quarries near Sylacauga. In the late 1830s, they became the first Alabamians to quarry marble and cut tombstones from the Sylacauga Marble Belt. Signed tombstones have been found for George Herd, the oldest brother to emigrate and the entrepreneur of the statewide business, and Alexander Herd, the second oldest brother. In the late 1840s, Alexander served as the proprietor of Eutaw Marble Works, which provided tombstones for western Alabama. The majority of the signed Mesopotamia tombstones bear a Herd signature.

George and Alexander Herd first arrived in the United States with fellow Scotsman Richard Miller. Miller and the Herds partnered to purchase marble quarries and advertised the sale of tombstones as early as 1838. When brothers David, John, and Thomas Herd arrived from Scotland to join the family business in 1842, Miller moved to Columbus, Mississippi, and formed Columbus Marble Works with his brother Cornelius. The Miller business still operates in Mississippi, manufacturing monuments and markers, while the Herd operation ended with Alexander's death in the late 1870s.

Though this chapter focuses primarily on the work of the Herd brothers, there are a number of additional 19th-century carver signatures in Mesopotamia, including the following: T. H. Wildman, Tuska; Barret & Co. N. O. [New Orleans]; T. H. Holt, Birmingham; Rosebrough and Sons, St. Louis; A. J. Yancey, Corinth, Mississippi; McDonald, March & Co., Mobile; and O'Neil, Meridian, Mississippi.

MARBLE READY FOR SHIPPING, SYLACAUGA. Deemed "the Marble City," Sylacauga is constructed on a solid deposit of the hardest, whitest, purest marble in the world. The bed is approximately 32 miles long by 1.5 miles wide and 400 feet deep. The quarries in Sylacauga provided much of the marble used for tombstones throughout Greene County. (Library of Congress, Prints and Photographs Division, HAER-ALA, 61-SYLA.V, 5-8.)

GANTT QUARRY, TALLADEGA COUNTY. Dr. Edward F. Gantt reputedly first discovered Alabama marble on his farm just south of Sylacauga in 1820. The Gantt quarry changed ownership a number of times and is currently owned by Imerys, "the world's largest producer of white industrial minerals." (Alabama Department of Archives and History, Montgomery.)

TOMBSTONE SIGNED BY RICHARD AND CORNELIUS MILLER, 1843. The Millers carved a coffin and flaming urn on the well-preserved marble headstone of Mary Dunlap (1768–1843). The coffin symbolizes mortality, but the flame suggests that the soul will continue to exist in the next realm. It is thought that the phrase "gone to pot" came from the use of the funerary urn. The stone is signed "R & C Miller, Col. Miss." In the late 1830s, Richard and Cornelius Miller emigrated from Scotland to Talladega County, where they jointly purchased marble quarries with the Herd brothers. In 1842, the Millers moved to Columbus, Mississippi, and started their own business called Columbus Marble Works. It is still in operation, producing "Artistic Memorials in Granite and Marble" and at one time manufacturing license plates as well.

GEORGE HERD, ENTREPRENEUR (1809–1855). The son of Alexander Herd and Margaret Martin, George was the eldest brother to emigrate from Scotland in the 1830s and the firm's business manager. His two sisters—Ann (b. 1807) and Jean (b. 1805)—and brother James (b. 1811) remained in Scotland. One of the Herds' earliest advertisements in Greene County appeared in the *Whig and Public Advertiser* in 1846 and stated that the business provided "Tombs, Monuments, Slabs, Head and Foot Stones, & c.—either of Italian or Talladega Marble." Herd tombstones can be found throughout Alabama; those with the earliest year of death (1833) are signed "G. Herd. Eutaw," while those with the latest year of death (1876) are signed "A. Herd, Birmingham." George, who died suddenly in 1855, is buried in the Old Syllacauga Cemetery in Talladega County. (B. B. Comer Memorial Library, Carolyn Lane Luttrell Collection.)

DAVID HERD (1819–1887). Born in Scotland on May 12, 1819, David is credited with the artistry in the family, as well as being the first to use Sylacauga marble for statuary purposes. David immigrated to the United States with his younger brothers John and Thomas in 1842, after he and John had completed their mason apprenticeship in Tibbermore, Perth, Scotland. Following George's death, Thomas returned to Scotland and died shortly thereafter at the age of 29. George W. Herd, the nephew of David Herd, stated in an interview, "The Herds said that the Marble Valley Stone and the Hickman Quarry stone were too soft," possibly explaining why the brothers stopped using Talladega marble. This statement was confirmed in an 1860 *Eutaw Independent Observer* advertisement placed by Alexander Herd that "would inform the public that he uses no Talladega marble—nothing but ITALIAN and Vermont Marble used." David and John Herd are buried in the Old Sylacauga Cemetery in Talladega County. (B. B. Comer Memorial Library, Carolyn Lane Luttrell Collection.)

TOMBSTONE SIGNED BY G. HERD. Abraham Flinn, a 3rd corporal in the Eutaw Rangers, was injured in Camargo during the Mexican War. Discharged with a surgeon's certificate of disability on December 20, 1846, he headed to Eutaw to convalesce. Flinn was almost home when two of the boilers on the steamboat *Tuscaloosa* exploded, killing him at the age of 37.

TOMBSTONE RECEIPT DATED APRIL 12, 1849. The Herd brothers generally divided the work between them, with "artist" David Herd more than likely the carver of the Masonic emblems at a cost of $20. John Herd "could cut more letters in a day" and was probably responsible for the lettering at a rate of 5¢ each. (Greene County Courthouse, estate file of Abraham Flinn.)

September 28 th 1863.

Dear Lela we bend over thy tomb
And mourn thy early doom
That all our tears and prayers
Could not save thee from the
conquering grave.

LELA HERD. Alexander Herd married Margaret Hamlett, the daughter of William Hamlett and Sarah Anderson, in Greene County in 1853. Alexander and Margaret had three children while living in Eutaw: Lela (1854–1863), William (1856–1936), and Jennie Lee (1862–1934). After his brother George died in 1855, Alexander, the second eldest, became the business manager of the marble operation. Business receipts dated 1855 and later were recorded as "Alexander Herd and Brothers," though the operation in Eutaw was called Eutaw Marble Works. Lela, who died at age nine, is buried in Mesopotamia Cemetery. One can imagine Alexander's state of mind as he carved the following inscription on his daughter's tombstone: "Dear Lela we bend over thy tomb / And mourn thy early doom / That all our tears and prayers / Could not save thee from the / conquering grave."

HERD RESIDENCE, LITTLEBERRY PIPPEN HOUSE. In December 1853, Alexander Herd purchased a house on Springfield Street in Eutaw for his expanding family. The Springfield Street residence still stands and is now listed on the National Register of Historic Places as the Littleberry Pippen House. Alexander also bought two city lots on the town square where Eutaw Marble Works was likely first located. (Greene County Historical Society.)

HERD RESIDENCE, VAUGHN-MORROW HOUSE. Alexander sold the Pippen House and the city lots and purchased another historic home, known as the Iredell P. Vaughn house, on Main Street in Eutaw. During the Reconstruction era of the 1870s, he sold this house at about one-third of its original price, and his family relocated to Birmingham.

EUTAW PRESBYTERIAN CHURCH, ERECTED 1851. When Alexander Herd purchased the Vaughn-Morrow house at 310 Main Street and lots 76–79, he relocated the marble business. Eutaw Marble Works was situated behind the Eutaw Presbyterian Church on Main Street in Eutaw, which was an excellent place for garnering business. The church was first organized in 1824 under the name Mesopotamia Presbyterian Church. The original whale oil lamps, manufactured by Cornelius and Company, are still in use, though they have since been converted to electric. The church is well maintained with an active congregation and is listed on the National Register of Historic Places. The historic marker at the church reads, "Eutaw, Alabama. Erected 1851, D. R. Anthony Contractor. Organized by Tuscaloosa Presbytery in 1824 as Mesopotamia Presbyterian Church. John H. Gray first minister 1826–1836. Educational Building Erected 1959." (Library of Congress, Prints and Photographs Division, HABS-ALA, 31-EUTA-10-1.)

TOMBSTONE SIGNED BY A. HERD, 1855. The tombstone of Anderson Greenwood, a Civil War soldier who died in the service of his country in Lynchburg, Virginia, is an intricately carved white marble slab with the signature "A. Herd" in the bottom right corner. Alexander's unique trademark, which divides the inscription and the epitaph, can sometimes be used to initially identify his stones when a signature is lacking. Many of his tombstones bear thoughtful, personalized inscriptions, as does this one when Alexander uses Greenwood's nickname in the first line: "Houston thou art gone to rest." It is not known where Alexander Herd and his wife are buried; however, evidence indicates that they are in Eutaw. It is probable that they were interred in Mesopotamia near their daughter Lela and their tombstones have just long since disappeared. Perhaps if Alexander had commissioned his own tombstone it would still be standing.

PHILLIP SCHOPPERT, UNDERTAKER AND CARPENTER. Alexander Herd carved the tombstones for his business associate Phillip Schoppert (1800–1871) and his wife, Mary (1804–1869). Phillip was the son of George Schoppert and Catherine Waters of Newberry District, South Carolina. Early advertisements indicate that he worked as an undertaker, sold metallic burial cases and wooden coffins, and furnished a hearse when desired.

R. P. SCHOPPERT, DEALER IN FURNITURE AND UNDERTAKER. Phillip Schoppert's sons Robert P. (1835–1913) and Patrick C. (1838–1881) acquired the concern and advertised frequently in the local papers, stating their business as "Undertaker and Builder, Dealer in Furniture of all kinds—will also take orders for tombstones and monuments of all kinds." Both sons are buried in Mesopotamia Cemetery. (Greene County Courthouse, estate file of W. P. Byrd.)

TOMBSTONE SIGNED BY A. J. YANCEY. A. J. Yancey of Corinth, Mississippi, and later Birmingham, Alabama, signed this marble tombstone for Alma (no surname). The inscription indicates that Alma died on her 12th birthday, September 28, 1883, and the lamb, frequently used for children's tombstones, symbolizes innocence. The curious thing is the epitaph: "Respect the resting place of the friendless."

TOMBSTONE SIGNED BY MCDONALD, MARCH, AND COMPANY. Thomas McDonald purchased the marble business of Mobile carver Jarvis Turner and then teamed with marble yard owner Richard March to form McDonald, March, and Company, a very successful tombstone firm based in Mobile County, Alabama. The tombstone of Julia Perkins, the wife of S. P. Watson, is signed "McDonald, March & Co., Mobile."

Three

SOUTHERN CROSS
OF HONOR

Many Greene County fathers and sons are buried in Mesopotamia, their tombstones engraved with the Southern Cross of Honor, a military decoration meant to honor soldiers for their valor in the armed forces of the Confederate States of America during the Civil War. The Ladies Memorial Association erected a Confederate monument in Mesopotamia Cemetery in the early 1900s in observation of Greene County's Confederate veterans, and as a tribute to the unnamed Confederate dead, a row of cast-iron Southern Crosses of Honor were placed along the west side of the cemetery.

In 1864, Samuel W. Dunlap, the mayor of Eutaw, sent out a plea to Greene County citizens "to come forward immediately and raise a fund for defraying the expenses of sick and wounded soldiers arriving in the town." The newspaper's editor reported, "Heretofore the burden of meeting these demands has fallen on a few persons living, or having offices of business, immediately around the public square." Though wives, mothers, and sisters mourned their losses, they pulled together as only a small community can to lend aid to the cause. The patriotic ladies of outlying communities responded quickly, raising funds with a "Musical Soiree" described as a "rich musical feast" in the small town of Pleasant Ridge, with other towns expected to follow their lead.

While Confederate soldiers comprise the majority of the early military burials, interments also include soldiers from the War of 1812 and the Mexican War. The Eutaw Rangers were organized in Greene County under the leadership of Col. Sydenham Moore and 1st Lt. Stephen Fowler Hale. The company spent 12 months in service during the Mexican War, returning to Greene County in June 1847. Eight Eutaw Rangers are buried in Mesopotamia: Pvt. William A. Bell, Pvt. James F. Cross, Pvt. Patrick Daly, 3rd Corp. Abram Flinn, 1st Corp. Beverly Greenwood, 1st Lt. Stephen F. Hale, Pvt. Simeon A. Maxwell, and Pvt. Isaac Oliver. Both Sydenham Moore and Stephen Fowler Hale subsequently lost their lives in service during the Civil War.

JOHN JONES WINSTON, WAR OF 1812 VETERAN (1785–1850). The son of Revolutionary War captain Anthony Winston and Keziah Jones of Virginia, John Jones Winston served as a captain in Coffee's Regiment during the War of 1812. His eldest brother Anthony was a lieutenant, and five of his brothers contributed to the ranks of Winston's Company from Madison County, Alabama. John served as an Alabama state representative in 1835. (Greene County Historical Society.)

MASONIC ACRONYM. John Jones Winston, his son John Milton Winston, and his grandson John James Winston were Royal Arch Masons, as indicated by the symbols carved on their tombstones. The letters HTWSSTKS, serving as an acronym for "Hiram the Widow's Son Sent to King Solomon," are etched in a keystone for Royal Arch Masons.

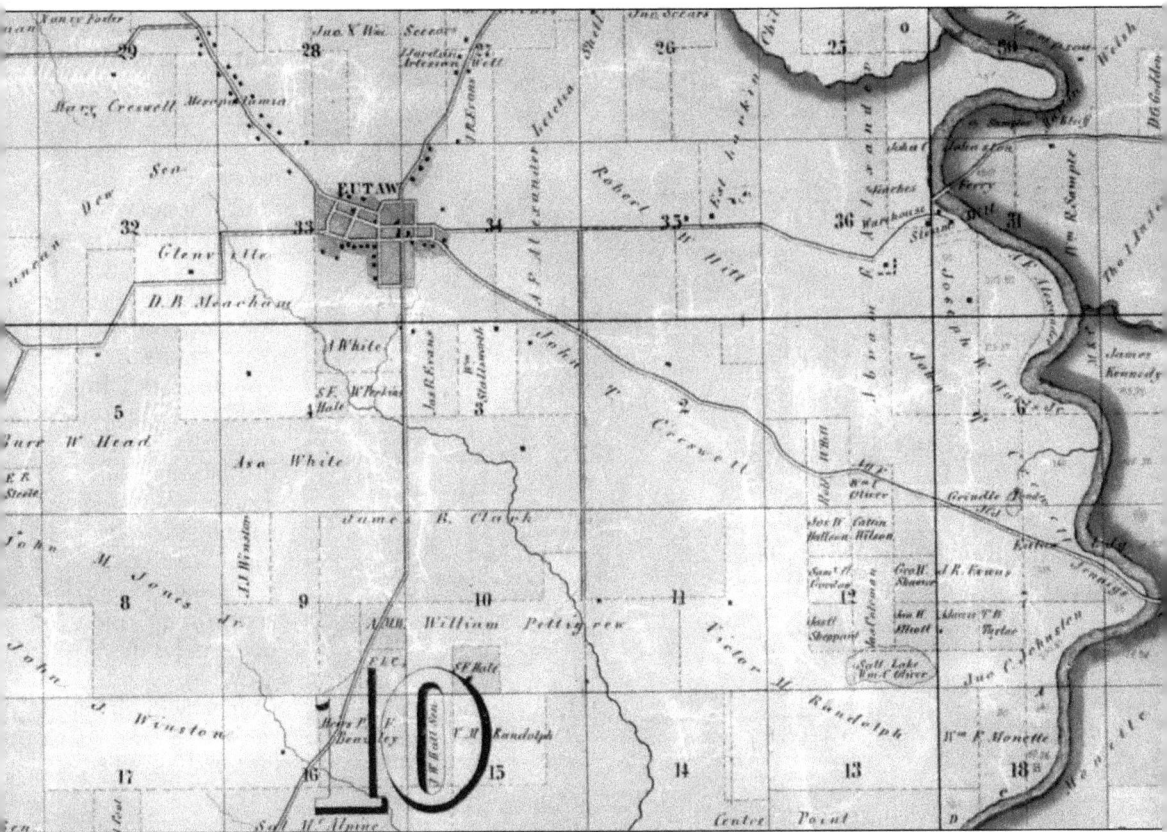

WINSTON LAND, SOUTH OF EUTAW. The Winstons owned an extensive cotton plantation in Eutaw (lower left corner), as well as land on the Black Warrior River for warehousing their cotton. The following was reported in the *Alabama Beacon* on October 12, 1843: "We have seen a statement of a Cotton-picking, on the farm of Col. John J. WINSTON, of this county, which beats anything in that line we have ever recorded. We have not space to give more than a brief abstract of the statement. THORNTON picked 428 lbs. in one day—JIM 413 lbs.—MAC and BEN, each, 387 lbs.—HENRY 378 lbs.—DAN 330 lbs. . . . This is a picking which any of our planters may be safely challenged to beat. . . . So here will be a yield of about 1800 or 2000 lbs. per acre. This we call good cropping and good picking. Beat it who can, in the county or in the State." (Alabama Department of History and Archives, Montgomery.)

COL. JOHN MILTON WINSTON (1808–1847). The eldest son of John Jones Winston and Mary Francis "Polly" Jones was born in Nashville, Tennessee. John Milton Winston was a commission merchant in business with John Anthony Winston, the 15th governor of Alabama. John Anthony Winston, a nephew of John Jones Winston, established the cotton commission house of John A. Winston and Company in Mobile in 1844.

HOME OF LUCY NORFLEET WINSTON (1860–1937) AND MARY "JOHNNIE" WINSTON (1862–1942). Lucy and Johnnie were the daughters of John James and Mary Virginia (McAlpine) Winston. Their 1880 Victorian house on Wilson Street in Eutaw is featured in *The Walking and Driving Guide to Historic Eutaw, Alabama.* Mary Virginia, Lucy, and Johnnie were all interred in Mesopotamia Cemetery. (Greene County Historical Society.)

LOT OF COL. JOSEPH PICKENS (1791–1853). The youngest son of Gen. Andrew Pickens and Rebecca Floride Calhoun, Joseph married Caroline J. Henderson (1807–1993), the daughter of John D. and Elizabeth Henderson. The Pickens family lot is located in a fenced area underneath a large magnolia tree in Mesopotamia Cemetery. Pickens County, Alabama, and Pickens County, South Carolina, were both named in honor of Gen. Andrew Pickens.

COL. JOSEPH PICKENS, AN HONEST MAN. Colonel Pickens was born at the family home in Hopewell, Pendleton District, South Carolina. The epitaph on his marble tombstone reads, "Youngest Son of Genl. Andrew Pickens; Born Mar. 30th 1791; Died Feb'y. 3rd 1853; In honors path he firmly trod. And liv'd & died the noblest work of God. An honest Man."

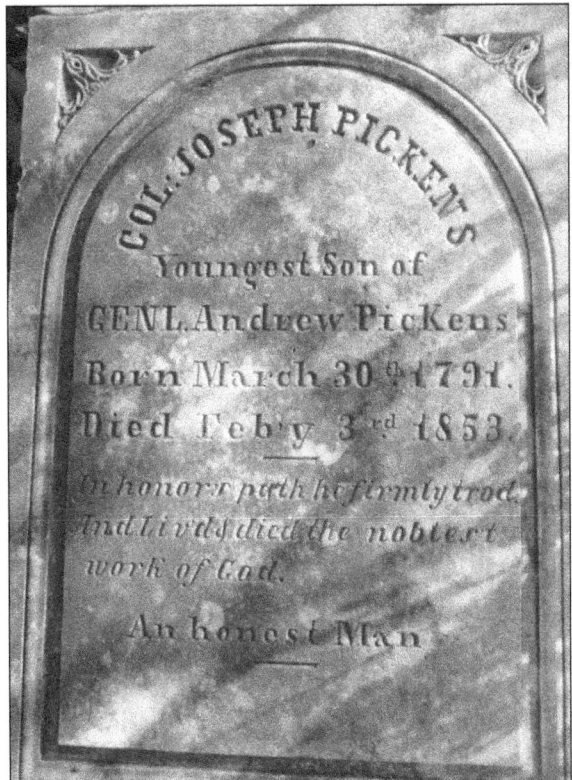

35

RECEIPT FOR CLOTHING. This 1848 receipt indicates that the Pickens family was quite well off. Caroline Pickens purchased a hat for $200, two and one-quarter yards of lacy cloth for $400, and pants, coat, and vest for $800. Colonel Pickens worked as a commission merchant with his son-in-law Duff Green. Their firm, Pickens and Green, brokered cotton out of offices in Mobile, Alabama. (Deborah Stone.)

PICKENS PLACE, EUTAW. Pickens Place was built for Joseph and Caroline Pickens in 1843. Copies of letters that Caroline wrote in the 1860s, as well as original receipts and Joseph's will, were found in the attic and remain in the home today. The residence has been converted to a popular bed and breakfast called Oakmont. (Deborah Stone.)

GEN. JOHN MCQUEEN (1804–1867). Gen. John McQueen was born to Col. James and Ann (McRae) McQueen of Queensdale, North Carolina, in 1804. He first married Sarah Rogers and had one son, Sarius Francis McQueen. After the death of his first wife, John married Sarah Pickens of Eutaw. He graduated from the University of North Carolina at Chapel Hill, studied law, and was admitted to the bar in 1828. He served in Congress from 1849 until 1860, when he became a member of the Confederate Congress for four years. A secessionist of the first order, John was conferred the title of general by the legislature of South Carolina when he was elected and commissioned commander-in-chief of the state militia. General McQueen died at his home in Society Hill, South Carolina, and is buried in the Episcopal Cemetery of Society Hill. (*The MacQueens of Queensdale.*)

SARAH PICKENS MCQUEEN (1831–1909). The daughter of Col. Joseph Pickens and Caroline Henderson and the granddaughter of Gen. Andrew Pickens, Sarah was the second wife of Gen. John McQueen of South Carolina. According to the book, *The MacQueens of Queensdale*, she reportedly "traveled extensively, mingling with the Nation's learned and great of both sexes, with a voice that characterized the cultured woman of the Old South." The McQueens had five children: Caroline (died in infancy), Joseph Pickens, Flora (died in infancy), John, and James William. Gen. John and Sarah Pickens McQueen lost their South Carolina home and possessions to fire during the Civil War. Sarah brought her three young sons back to Eutaw after the death of her husband in 1867. The two eldest sons, Joseph Pickens McQueen (1854–1904) and John McQueen (1863–1921), are both buried in Mesopotamia. (*The MacQueens of Queensdale.*)

COL. SYDENHAM MOORE, EUTAW RANGER AND CONFEDERATE ARMY OFFICER (1817–1862).
Moore attended the University of Alabama and practiced law, serving as probate judge of Greene
County until the Mexican War. Moore commanded Company D, 1st Regiment of Alabama
Volunteers, also known as the Eutaw Rangers, during the Mexican War and then returned to
Greene County, again serving as probate judge. Elected to Congress in 1857, he resigned when
Alabama seceded from the Union. Moore and fellow Greene Countian Stephen F. Hale were
killed in action as officers in the Confederate States Army, 11th Alabama Infantry, Company B.
In May 1862, he was mortally wounded at the Battle of Seven Pines near Richmond, Virginia.
He died in August and was buried in the New Greensboro Cemetery in Hale County. Moore was
photographed at Matthew Brady's Washington studio in 1858. (W. S. Hoole Special Collections
Library, University of Alabama.)

STEPHEN FOWLER HALE, EUTAW RANGER AND CONFEDERATE ARMY OFFICER (1816–1862). Hale was born in Crittenden County, Kentucky, and graduated from the law department at Transylvania University. He practiced law in Eutaw until 1843, when he was elected to the legislature. Hale married Mary Kirksey before joining the Eutaw Rangers and serving in the Mexican War as a 1st lieutenant. After returning from the war, Hale practiced law with partner Thomas C. Clark in the law firm of Hale and Clark, "Attorneys at Law and Solicitors in Chancery." Along with Col. Syndenham Moore, he commanded the 11th Regiment of Alabama Volunteers during the Civil War. After Moore's death, Lt. Col. Hale took command of the regiment and died in Virginia on July 18, 1862, from wounds received in the Battle of Gaines' Mill. A Grand Master Mason, Hale was awarded a gold medal by the Grand Lodge of Alabama for his service; it was presented to his wife since he did not survive the war. (Alabama Department of Archives and History, Montgomery.)

STEPHEN FOWLER HALE, STATESMAN, JURIST, PATRIOT, SOLDIER, AND CHRISTIAN GENTLEMAN. Hale County was named in honor of Lt. Col. Stephen Fowler Hale, an officer with the Eutaw Rangers during the Mexican War and a Confederate officer during the Civil War. Hale represented his district in the provisional congress of the Confederate States of America and served in the 11th Alabama Infantry.

PVT. BEVERLY GREENWOOD, EUTAW RANGER (1811–1852). Beverly Greenwood married Harriet R. Anderson, the daughter of Nathan and Margaret Anderson. Beverly, Harriet, and their sons Anderson "Houston" and Nathan K. Greenwood are buried in Mesopotamia. Both Houston and Nathan died during service in the Civil War. Beverly's tombstone is signed by Alexander Herd.

41

ISAAC OLIVER, EUTAW RANGER (1820–1862). Born in Nottoway, Virginia, Isaac Oliver died in Greene County at the age of 42. Oliver married Julia L. Murphy and served as county sheriff in 1856. A 4th corporal with the Eutaw Rangers, he was discharged at Camargo, Mexico, on a surgeon's certificate of disability.

WILLIAM A. BELL, ESQUIRE, EUTAW RANGER (1821–1846). Bell was born in Greene County and died during the Mexican War in Matamoras, Mexico, on Christmas Day in 1846. His remains were returned for burial at Mesopotamia. Bell was described as "the pride of his friends—the soul of the social circle—one of nature's noblemen—magnanimous, generous, and kind."

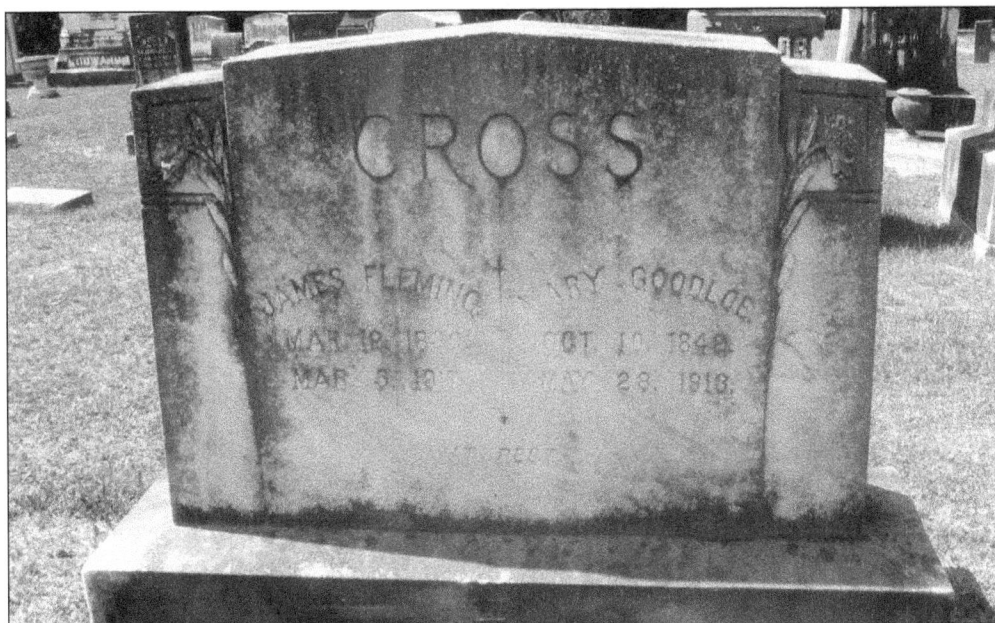

LT. JAMES FLEMING CROSS (1830–1917). James Fleming Cross served with the Eutaw Rangers and as a 1st lieutenant in Company C, 11th Alabama Infantry, Confederate States Army. James was born at Mount Pleasant in Murray County, Tennessee, the son of Joseph Oliver Cross and Eliza Harlan Cross. He first married Margaret Rose Dunlap (1831–1871), and after her death, he wed Mary Elizabeth Goodloe (1848–1913.)

JAMES FLEMING CROSS (LEFT) AND JEHU "HUGH" CROSS. Brothers James and Hugh are pictured at the Clinton home of their stepbrother John Baskin Dunlap. In addition to James, Joseph and Eliza had four children: Sarah Ann (b. 1828), Hugh (b. 1832), Isabella (b. 1835), and Elizabeth (b. 1838). (Clinton Cross.)

LT. JAMES FLEMING CROSS. When he was 16 years old, James joined the Eutaw Rangers with his stepbrother Pleasant Tannehill. William Tannehill, the second husband of James's mother, Eliza Harlan, was the brother of Ninian Tannehill, who owned Tannehill Ironworks southwest of Birmingham. William Tannehill was killed when the boilers exploded on the steamboat *Tuscaloosa* in 1847. Margaret Rose Dunlap, the daughter of John and Elizabeth Dunlap, was the first wife of Lt. James Fleming Cross. The couple had eight children: John Baskin, Walter J., Estelle, Alice, Ewell F., Ed, Oliver H., and James F. Lt. James Fleming Cross and his second wife, Mary Elizabeth Goodloe, had five children: Mattie L., French G., Fleming L., Mary K., Cora, and Kate H. (Clinton Cross.)

MAJ. GEN. DANIEL HAMMOND BYRD (1807–1865). Daniel Hammond Byrd commanded the 12th Division of the Georgia Militia during the Mexican War and enlisted in the Greene County local militia during the Civil War. He was one of the earliest settlers of Cherokee County, Georgia, descending from Revolutionary War patriot John Byrd. Daniel's sons—Alexander H., William P., and Winfield S. Byrd—are also buried in Mesopotamia.

HOME OF LT. WINFIELD SCOTT BYRD. Winfield purchased this home on Mesopotamia Street in 1869. Built with materials salvaged from the Mesopotamia Church, it is listed on the National Register of Historic Places. Winfield, a schoolteacher, enlisted in Company B, 11th Alabama Infantry, in June 1861 as a private and was promoted to lieutenant. (Fenwick Campbell Bird.)

The Est of W. P. Bird for Burial
Eutaw, Ala., May 30 1891

BOUGHT OF **EUTAW MERCANTILE CO.,**
WHOLESALE AND RETAIL DEALERS IN

GENERAL MERCHANDISE.

1891

MARKET PRICE PAID FOR COTTON AND COUNTRY PRODUCE.

May	6	1 Suit Clothes 15.00	1 Shirt 1.50	16	50	
		1 Under Shirt 50	1 Pr Drawers 75	1	25	
		1 Pr 1/2 Hose 40	1 Pr Cuffs 30		70	
		1 Collar 25	1 Tie 25		50	
		1 Pr Shoes 1.25	5 Collar Button 25	1	50	$20.45

Paid by Miss A M Byrd
Sept 15/91

Eutaw Mercantile Co
Per A T Sexton

WILLIAM P. BYRD (1841–1891).
Annie Mary Bird (or Byrd), the administrator for the William P. Byrd estate, purchased new clothing from the Eutaw Mercantile Company in which to bury her brother. William served in Company B, 11th Alabama Infantry, Confederate States Army. (Greene County Courthouse, estate file of W. P. Byrd.)

WILLIAM P. BYRD LOT. In 1864, the *Eutaw Whig and Observer* reported the following: "Our gallant young friend William Bird is, we are pleased to know, rapidly recovering from the wound which he received in the battle of Spotsylvania, C. H. This brave young man enlisted in the first company raised in our county, was in all the great Virginia and Maryland battles and behaved in them all with the most distinguished gallantry."

DR. ALEXANDER H. BYRD (1849–1904). Dr. Byrd operated his medical practice in an office near the Episcopal church on Mesopotamia Street in Eutaw. He and his wife, Julia W. (Blocker) Byrd, raised nine children and resided at the Greene County plantation known as Hohenlinden, located southwest of Eutaw.

DR. BYRD RECEIPT. This receipt, from the estate file of William P. Byrd, is for services to Dr. A. H. Byrd, the son of Gen. Daniel H. Byrd. (Greene County Courthouse, estate file of W. P. Byrd.)

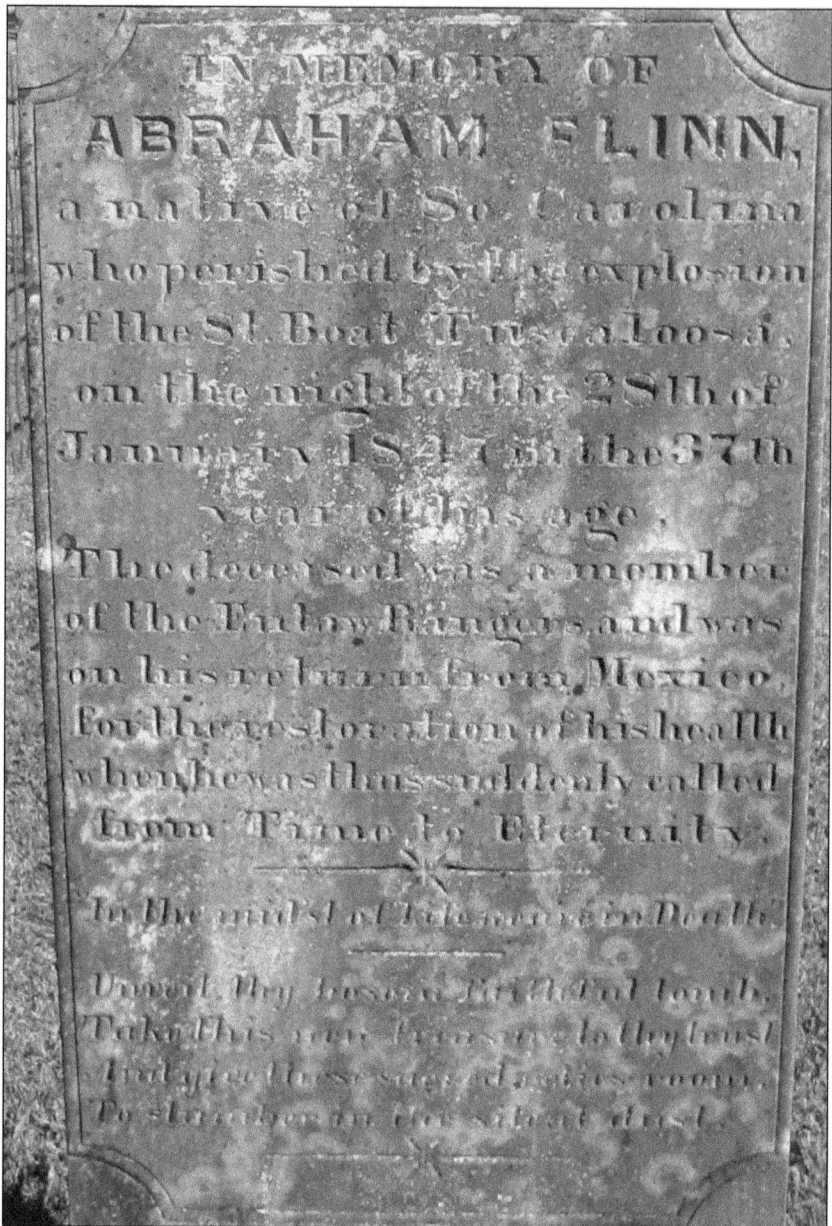

ABRAHAM FLINN, 3RD CORPORAL. In November 1846, 3rd Corp. Abraham Flinn took ill while the Eutaw Rangers were stationed at Camargo, Mexico. Conditions in the camps, notoriously poor, were described by one soldier in a letter home: "Premature death was brought on by disease, the result of poor sanitation, exposure to the elements, the crowding in which germs could rapidly spread, or a combinations of all three." Flinn was discharged on a surgeon's certificate of disability and sent home. On the final leg of the trip, he started up the Black Warrior River aboard the steamboat *Tuscaloosa*. His epitaph tells the story: "Abraham Flinn, a native of So. Carolina who perished by the explosion of the St. Boat Tuscaloosa on the night of the 28th of January 1847 in the 37th year of his age. The deceased was a member of the Eutaw Rangers and was on his return from Mexico for the restoration of his health when he was thus suddenly called from time to eternity."

MEMORIAL PLAQUE, APRIL 26, 1937. The first Greene County chapter of the United Daughters of the Confederacy (UDC) was organized in 1911 by Jane DuBois (Monroe) Rutherford. The chapter was named in honor of her father, William O. Monroe, owner and editor of the *Whig and Observer* newspaper. Mrs. Rutherford (1869–1919) is buried in Mesopotamia next to her son William O. Rutherford (1902–1918.) In March 1921, the new Greene County chapter was founded. Addie McLemore, president of the Ladies Memorial Association, is credited with the placement of the Confederate monument in Mesopotamia Cemetery. Officers elected by ballot included president Addie McLemore, vice-president Mary F. Brodnax, recording secretary Mary Banks, historian Hattie Aldridge, registrar Lydie (Taylor) Eatman, chaplain Daisy (Meriwether) Dunlap, and treasurer Emma Skelton. The UDC traditionally placed a large wreath on the Confederate statue and decorated the graves of veterans with flowers each Memorial Day. The ladies also placed an attractive gate at the entrance to the cemetery, which has since disappeared.

DR. JOHN SAMUEL MERIWETHER (1830–1879). The son of Dr. Willis Meriwether and Judah Pollard Chiles, Dr. John Samuel Meriwether served in the 38th and 40th Alabama Infantry Regiments and as head surgeon of the Confederate Hospital at Eufaula, Alabama, with the rank of major. His wife, Alice Coleman (1839–1919), the daughter of James Cobb Coleman and Juliet Bestor Coleman, is buried next to him.

MERIWETHER HOUSE, RELOCATED FROM SPRINGFIELD. The Meriwether House, listed on the National Register of Historic Places, was reconstructed in 1856 and may be all that is remaining of the now-defunct village of Springfield. According to family oral tradition, the house was "at Springfield and brought to Eutaw." Springfield, located three miles northeast of Eutaw, flourished between 1825 and 1838, boasting large stores and two hotels. (Greene County Historical Society.)

WILLIAM CARPENTER STORE, CLINTON. Many Greene County Civil War soldiers signed up for duty in small stores spread throughout the county such as the Carpenter Store in Clinton. Clinton was a fairly large and active community, located about eight miles northwest of Eutaw, until a major fire in April 1904 destroyed most of the buildings, including the store pictured above. (Clinton Cross.)

OVERVIEW OF THE CLARK LOT. James and Mary Clark were the parents of seven sons and two daughters, eight of which are buried in Mesopotamia. The Clarks saw five sons off to war with the Confederate States Army. James traveled to Virginia to recover the bodies of his two sons who did not survive the war and returned them to Greene County for burial in Mesopotamia Cemetery.

JAMES BLAIR CLARK, FATHER OF FIVE CIVIL WAR SOLDIERS (1796–1873). James Blair Clark practiced law and became a representative in the Alabama legislature from 1827 to 1831. He moved to Eutaw in the 1830s and practiced law until 1845, when he was appointed the Greene County chancellor. His first wife, Mary Erwin (1804–1863), was the sister of Hon. John Erwin of Greensboro.

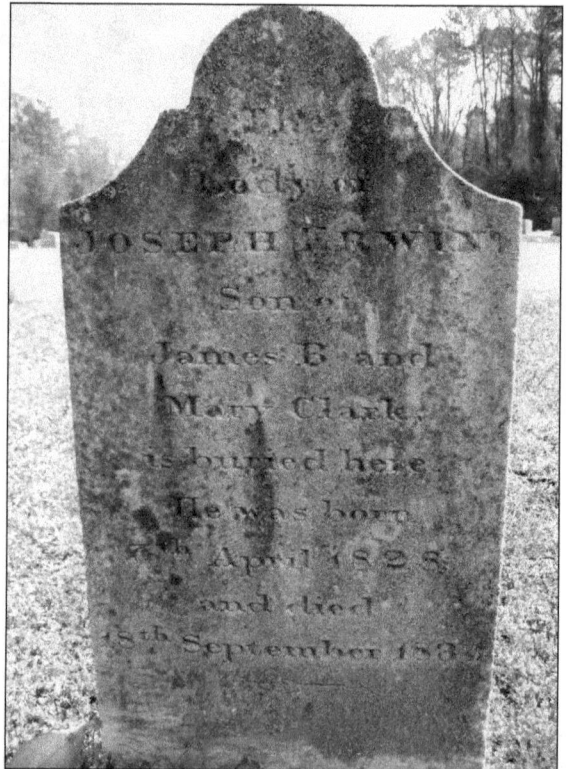

JOSEPH ERWIN CLARK (1828–1834). The Clarks lost their second eldest son, Joseph Erwin Clark, at the age of six and their eldest daughter, Mary Erwin Clark (1844–1862), to typhoid fever at the age of 17. Joseph was one of the earliest burials in Mesopotamia Cemetery.

GENERAL BUTLER'S HEADQUARTERS, FRASER'S FARM, NORTH SIDE OF JAMES RIVER. Henry Clay Clark, the sixth son of James and Mary Clark, was born on December 3, 1838, in Cahaba, Dallas County, Alabama. Clay received a bachelor's degree at the University of Alabama. He died from wounds received at Fraser's Farm near Richmond, Virginia, on June 30, 1862. (Library of Congress, Prints and Photographs Division, Civil War Photographs, LC-USZ62-119935.)

MAIN EASTERN THEATER OF WAR, THE PENINSULAR CAMPAIGN, MAY–AUGUST 1862. Capt. James Davis Clark, the fourth son of James and Mary Clark, was born on May 11, 1833, and died at Richmond, Virginia, on July 3, 1862, from a wound received in the Seven Days Battle. Captain Clark's father traveled to Virginia to retrieve his body for burial at Mesopotamia. (Library of Congress, Prints and Photographs Division, Civil War Photographs, LC-B811- 2486.)

JOSEPH PICKENS CLARK. Born the fifth son of James and Mary Clark on January 29, 1836, Joseph Pickens Clark entered the service at Lynchburg, Virginia, in 1861 as a private in Company B, 11th Alabama Regiment, and continued until August 1862, when he was discharged after the loss of a hand. "Pickens" and his brother George were both injured during the Seven Days Battle at Gaines' Mill. (Frank Clark Parkins.)

POYNOR LOT. Capt. Digges Poynor (1835–1916), the son of Digges Poynor Sr. and Eliza Clifton Caroline Purdy, was born in Lawrenceville, Virginia, on November 14, 1835. A renowned educator, he wed Mary Eleanor Jones (1848–1936), the daughter of Henry G. Jones and Sara Kennedy, and raised nine children.

CAPT. DIGGES POYNOR. An 1860 graduate of the Virginia Military Institute, Captain Poynor served as instructor of military tactics at the University of Alabama from 1861 to 1865. He joined General Forrest's troops in Marion after the burning of the University of Alabama. Captain Poynor was attached to the Cadet Troops Company F, 7th Alabama Cavalry. (W. S. Hoole Special Collections, University of Alabama.)

COL. C. H. TAYLOR (1810–1892). Colonel Taylor, the son of Green Berry and Elizabeth Taylor, was born in Tennessee and went on to marry Nancy Dew (1824–1892), also buried in Mesopotamia. Taylor's draped marble monument is one of the largest in Mesopotamia, perhaps due to his successful merchandising business. The Dews were large plantation owners in the area.

55

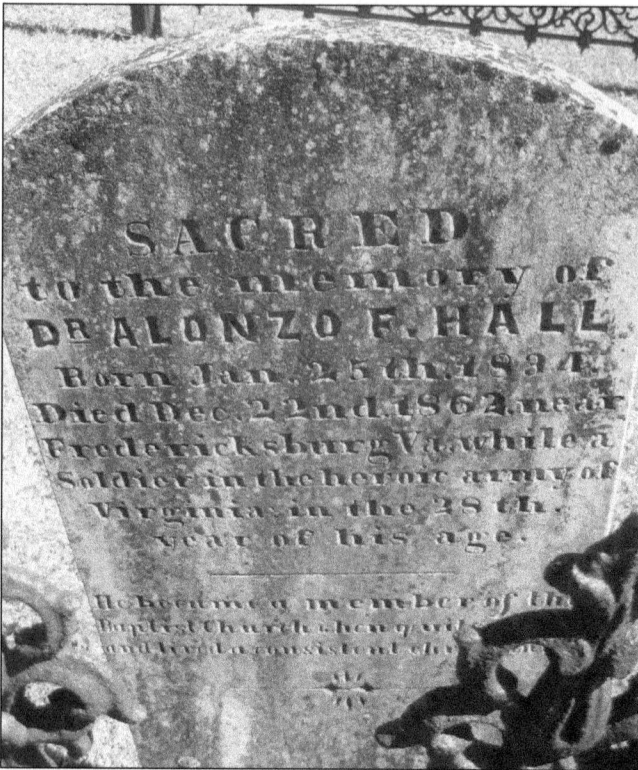

ALONZO F. HALL, D.D.S (1834–1862). Eutaw dentist Alonzo Hall ran a practice in partnership with Dr. R. G. Hamill of Livingston. He served as a 2nd sergeant in Company I, 5th Alabama Infantry, Confederate States Army, and died while on duty near Fredericksburg, Virginia, on December 22, 1862. He is buried in the Hall lot, which is surrounded by a wrought-iron corn stalk and rose fence.

JOSEPH WHITE HALL, KEEPER OF THE PARAPET HOTEL (1793–1868). Joseph Hall saw three sons into Confederate service: Winter Payne Hall (1841–1879), 2nd lieutenant in Company A, 40th Regiment, Alabama Infantry, and sheriff of Greene County; Col. Josephus Marion Hall, Company I, 5th Regiment, Alabama Infantry; and Alonzo Hall. Joseph married Elvira Pugh (1801–1864), the daughter of Elijah Pugh.

Four

THE RECONSTRUCTION ERA

The burning of the courthouse on the town square was one of the more obvious instances of the perilous atmosphere in Eutaw after the Civil War. The apparent reason for the fire was to obliterate evidence accumulated for use in indictments against local residents. The county was approximately 68 percent African American, with many of the newly freed slaves not quite sure of their place in a changing society and white plantation owners not quite ready to let them be equal.

After the Reconstruction Acts of 1867 were passed by Congress, federal troops were dispatched to Eutaw to establish military rule. During this time, an event known to locals as the Dry Tortugas Affair occurred, sending seven local men to prison in Florida. Annoyed with a carpetbagger, the men had decided to teach him a lesson. They were convicted after a controversial military trial in Selma and sentenced to Fort Jefferson Prison at Dry Tortugas Island by May 1868. The men were pardoned a few months later, after Alabama was readmitted to the Union.

Another blatant incident occurred in March 1870 when a band of disguised men entered the Cleveland House in Eutaw, where 35-year-old Republican county solicitor Alexander Boyd slept. Boyd's awareness of Klan indiscretions, coupled with his political affiliations, made him a prime target for the "night riders." The "armed, disguised, white night riders" shot him several times in the head and then galloped off.

In October of the same year, amidst a volatile atmosphere fueled by the clandestine evening excursions, the Eutaw Riot occurred. A Republican rally at the town square attended by upwards of 2,000 African Americans went awry after Republican leader Charles Hays took the stand to thank the speakers. When the African Americans perceived harm to Hays, some drew knives; the whites raised guns. Federal troops were on hand to quickly end the riot, though there were casualties.

Greene County Courthouse, Built 1839. The first courthouse and jail were constructed on Eutaw's public square in 1839. The courthouse was set afire in 1868 to destroy evidence accumulated for use in indictments against local residents. The courthouse was then reconstructed to be "substantially the same" as the previous building. (Alabama Department of Archives and History, Montgomery.)

Frank Henry Mundy (1837–1896). The son of Thomas Mundy and Mattie Browning, Frank Mundy was born in Oxford, England. His father and grandfather were both professors at Oxford. Frank married Mary Elizabeth Jarvis, the daughter of Alexander Jarvis, and had three children: Frank Perrin Mundy, Mattie Browning Mundy, and Thomas Gustave Mundy. Frank, Mary, Frank Perrin, and Mattie are buried in Mesopotamia Cemetery.

Lt. Frank Henry Mundy. A lieutenant in Company B, 11th Alabama Regiment, Frank Henry Mundy was captured by Union forces at Gettysburg in 1863 and remained a prisoner until the end of the war. He was one of seven men sent to prison in Dry Tortugas Island after harassing a carpetbagger in 1868. The minutes of the Constitutional Convention of 1901 reveal that Judge Thomas W. Coleman mentioned the affair: "In that year we had our first experience at Eutaw under Military Rule. Some of our young people, viz: William Pettigrew, Frank Mundy, Hugh L. White, Thomas W. Roberts, James Steele, John Cullen and Samuel Strayhorn were sentenced to Dry Tortugas for a term of years. . . . Hill, who came from Connecticut, became quite insolent when called upon to settle a small account. The accused placed him upon a rail, carried him upon their shoulders a short distance and then released him. He was not injured in the least and there were no purposes to injure him." (Alabama Department of Archives and History, Montgomery.)

Sen. Charles Hays (1834–1879). Charles Hays, a Republican leader during the Reconstruction era, was one of the most visible political figures in Alabama in the decade following the Civil War. An unlikely Republican, he was raised amongst Democrats on a prominent, slave-holding plantation called Hays Mount. Educated at the famed Green Springs School under the tutelage of Henry Tutwiler, Hays was well prepared for further education at the University of Georgia and the University of Virginia at Charlottesville. John Witherspoon DuBose labeled Hays "the most active and turbulent of the scalawags" in his book *Alabama's Tragic Decade*. Due to Eutaw's turbulent atmosphere, Hays made a decision to refrain from speaking at a Republican rally in 1870. When Hays attempted to adjourn the meeting, however, a white man yanked him from the stand, sparking the blacks in attendance to pull knives and the whites to start shooting. The gunfire triggered a stampede among the African Americans as they scrambled for safety. (Library of Congress, Brady-Handy Photograph Collection.)

MYRTLE HILL, GREENE COUNTY, THE HOME OF CHARLES HAYS. Sen. Charles Hays, the son of George Hays and Anne Miller Beville, moved to Myrtle Hill at the age of 30 and died there of Bright's (kidney) disease 15 years later. A major in the Confederate States Army, he married Margaret Cornelia Minerva Ormand of Tuscaloosa in 1863. (Library of Congress, Prints and Photographs Division, HABS-ALA, 32-EUTA, 1-3.)

ANNA PARKER MCQUEEN (1878–1947). The daughter of Joseph Pickens McQueen and Roberta Kirksey, Anna married Charles Hays Jr., the son of Senator Hays. She is buried in Mesopotamia next to the couple's son, also named Charles (b. and d. 1909.) Senator Hays's grandparents Judith and Woodliff Beville of Virginia were interred in Mesopotamia as well.

ALEXANDER BOYD, ESQUIRE (1834–1879). Alexander Boyd, the Republican solicitor for Greene County, was shot to death at the Cleveland Hotel in Eutaw on the night of March 31, 1870. Boyd's determination to prosecute several local citizens for the murders of two African Americans is thought to be the reason behind the killing. His epitaph reads, "Murdered by the Ku Klux!!!"

JUDGE WILLIAM C. OLIVER (1816–1893). Probate judge William C. Oliver was forcibly removed from his Greene County office in 1870, when he refused to surrender to the new Republican judge, William Miller. Escorted to office by armed guards, Miller found a threatening Klan notice tacked to his door two weeks later.

Five

THE LEGACY OF EUTAW

Eutaw's antebellum homes offer a glimpse of the past, when cotton and steamboats ruled the rivers and Southern hospitality was as evident as the stately magnolias. As Eutaw merchants prospered, they aimed to surpass each other in the extravagance of their homes. Gracious and lavish pillared mansions were built by Capt. Edwin Reese, a carriage manufacturer; William Perkins, a dry goods merchant; George W. Shawver, the proprietor of the Parapet Hotel; and Foster Mark Kirksey, county sheriff and cotton broker. These and many more structures survived the Civil War and its aftermath, providing the opportunity to enjoy Greene County's pillared past today.

Eutaw was a bustling agricultural community relying on cotton crops and the Black Warrior River to transport goods to Mobile. In 1856, V. Gayle Snedecor, in *Snedecor's Greene County Directory*, described Eutaw as follows:

It is situated about three miles west of the Warrior River, has a populous section north and a wealthy one south of it. It is built on an elevated and healthy location; has about 1,200 inhabitants, a handsome Court House surrounded by a beautiful square, a substantial Jail, four Dry Goods, one Clothing, three Drug, one Confectionary, one Book and several Grocery stores; three Hotels and several boarding houses; two Carriage and one Harness Manufactory; two Presbyterian, one Episcopal, one Baptist and one Methodist Church; one Female Seminary and two Male Academies, and one Masonic and one Odd Fellow's Lodge. Two newspapers are published here "The Alabama Whig" (political) and "Independent Observer" (neutral).

DAVID R. ANTHONY, BUILDER AND ARCHITECT (1808–1871). The son of Daniel Anthony and Eve Rhinehard of North Carolina, David Anthony was the most noted of Eutaw's early builders. He married Rebecca Frances High, the daughter of William M. High. David and his sons William M. (1854–1871) and Eddie H. (1864–1884) are buried in Mesopotamia.

HOME OF DAVID R. ANTHONY. David Anthony built the home of his future father-in-law, William M. High, in nearby Forkland. After completing Rose Hill, David married High's daughter and began constructing his own home across the street from the Eutaw Presbyterian Church. He reportedly helped build the church, the Mesopotamia Female Seminary, and Kirkwood. (Library of Congress, Prints and Photographs Division, HABS-ALA, 32-EUTA, 6-1.)

PROF. HENRY P. HATFIELD (1802–1864).
Professor Hatfield was an early Mesopotamia settler, arriving in the late 1830s. He married Margaret Abigail Reed and had three daughters while living in South Carolina. His eldest daughter, Anne Browne Hatfield, and his second wife, Stella (Phelps) Hatfield, ran the Mesopotamia Female Seminary until Henry's death in 1864.

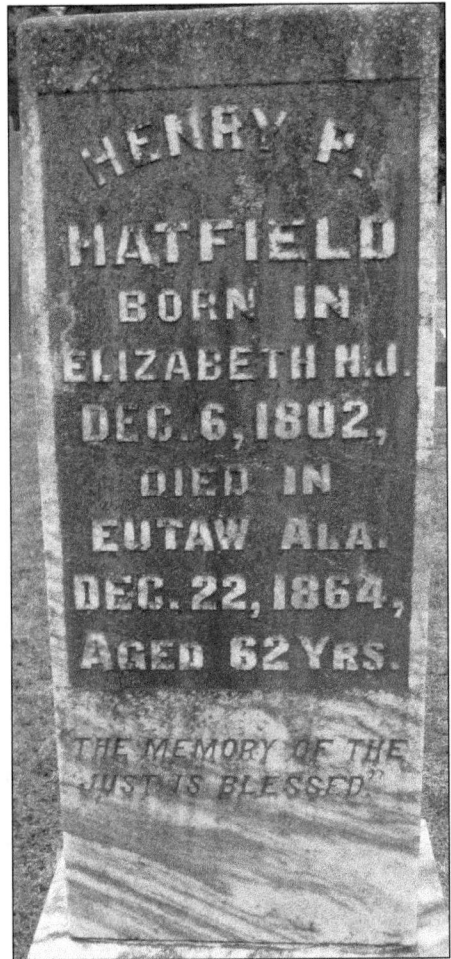

HENRY P. HATFIELD BORN IN ELIZABETH N.J. DEC. 6, 1802, DIED IN EUTAW ALA. DEC. 22, 1864, AGED 62 YRS. "THE MEMORY OF THE JUST IS BLESSED"

COMPOSED BY
Mrs. ANNE B. HATFIELD.
AND INSCRIBED TO THE PUPILS OF THE
MESOPOTAMIA FEMALE SEMINARY,
EUTAW, ALABAMA.

NEW YORK
PUBLISHED BY COOK & BRO. 343 BROADWAY.

THE MESOPOTAMIA WALTZ MAZURKA.
Anne Browne Hatfield composed this waltz for the pupils of the Mesopotamia Female Seminary in 1855. Anne; her husband, Abner A. Archibald; and her stepmother, Stella (Phelps) Hatfield, are buried in the Pleasant Ridge Cemetery in Greene County. Abner Archibald and his brother E. Addison Archibald established the Archibald Institute in Pleasant Ridge. (Greene County Historical Society.)

Entered according to Act of Congress in the Year 1855, by Cook & Bro. in the Clerk's Offic

MESOPOTAMIA FEMALE SEM

t of the Sⁿ D^r of N.Y.

MESOPOTAMIA FEMALE SEMINARY, EUTAW. Mr. and Mrs. Owen Meredith of Tuscaloosa presented this painting to the Greene County Library in 1937. The Mesopotamia Female Seminary was built on Mesopotamia Street near the cemetery in 1845. The 1847 board of trustees included Williamson A. Glover, Rev. Nicholas Ross Morgan, John W. Womack, John Coleman, and Col. Joseph Pickens. Mrs. P. M. Upson served as an early principal, while Rev. Nicholas Ross Morgan and his "lady" oversaw boarding at a cost of $10 per month, which included laundry services. The school offered basic subjects but also astronomy, Swift's philosophy, music (harp, piano, and guitar), orthography, French, and Latin. The building was moved to its present site in Eutaw in 1889, when it was acquired by the Eutaw Female College. (Greene County Historical Society.)

EUTAW HIGH SCHOOL AT THE OLD ACADEMY BUILDING, C. 1894. Kate Alexander (far left) taught at Eutaw High School from 1880 to 1911, when the new public school opened. Kate Alexander's school was located in the basement of the Presbyterian church until it moved to the above structure, owned by Judge Smith. (Greene County Historical Society.)

EUTAW SCHOOL, BUILT C. 1911. This institution opened on Eutaw Avenue in the fall of 1911, becoming the first public school with combined grades. The three-story brick building was of Renaissance architecture and was discontinued in 1920, when it failed to meet the necessary requirements for an Alabama public school. (Lee Ann Stuckey.)

GUSTAVE BRAUNE, SILVERSMITH (1822–1898). Gustave Maurice Braune, the son of Charles Frederick and Emily Seibert Braune, emigrated from Freiberg, Saxony, Germany, in 1836 at the age of 14. After hearing of the thriving town of Eutaw, he relocated to Greene County in 1856 from the Athens-Rome area of Georgia. He was the proprietor of G. Braune and Company, a jewelry shop on Prairie Street in Eutaw.

HONORIA THERESA (ROONEY) BRAUNE (1840–1873). The second wife of Gustave Braune, Honoria was born in Ireland in 1840 and died in Eutaw in 1873. Her beautiful, white marble tombstone depicts a Fleuree cross. Gustave and Honoria had three children: Helene Theresia (1867–1935), Margaret Augusta (1870–1921), and Gustave Monetz "Maurice" Braune (1872–1930).

GUSTAVE BRAUNE HOME, BUILT C. 1860. Gustave Braune purchased a one-room office in 1859 and expanded it to become a residence in 1860. Braune had returned from a trip to Germany with a model of a castle, which was used when designing the house's octagonal structure. Chris and Teresa (Inge) Beeker are the sixth generation of Braunes to live in the home. (Teresa Inge Beeker.)

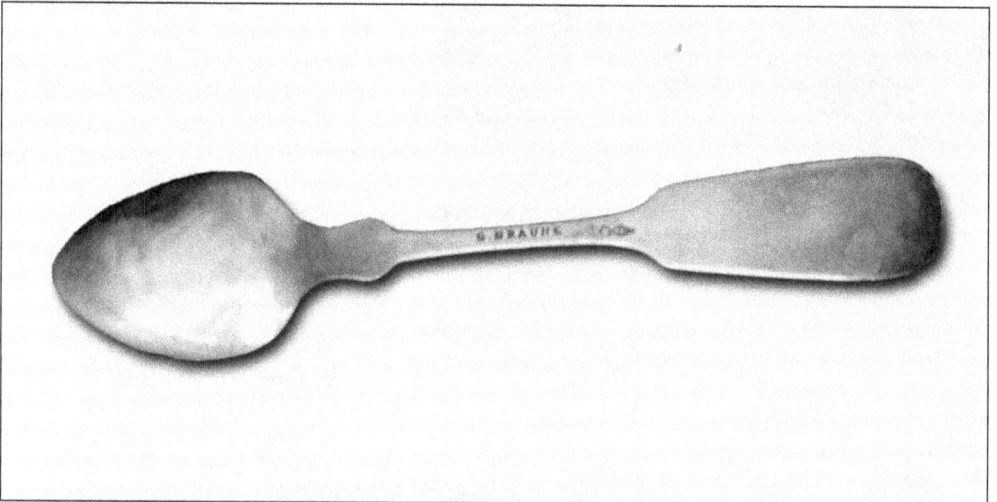

G. BRAUNE, COIN SILVER. This silver spoon, with the mark "G. Braune," is now a rare Southern coin silver collector's item. Braune made regular trips to New York to purchase the latest jewelry fashions, which he carried in his shop along with "a good stock of silver ware warranted to be coin silver." Braune also advertised the sale of watches, clocks, spectacles, chinaware, cutlery, and Colt pistols.

GUSTAVE BRAUNE PORTRAIT. Above the mantel in the dining room of the Braune home is one of many heirlooms that remain with descendants today: an oil portrait of Gustave Braune. The family also retained an impressive collection of silver pieces, jewelry, and gold-banded china once owned by Queen Charlotte of England.

GUSTAVE (LEFT IN DOORWAY) AND CHARLES H. BRAUNE (RIGHT IN DOORWAY) AT THE VIOLIN STUDIO. Gustave's brother Charles H. Braune taught piano and violin, having had a "long and varied course of study in the celebrated Music Schools of Germany." Professor Braune sold Steinway and Sons pianos, violins, guitars, and sheet music in addition to offering "piano tuning and repairing." (Teresa Inge Beeker.)

Rev. John DuBois. A manufacturer of cotton gins, Rev. John DuBois earned three patents on improvements made to the DuBois Cotton Gin. His innovations in design and operation are documented in U.S. Patent Office files and in various 19th-century issues of *Scientific American*. Reverend DuBois and his wife, Louisa, both buried in Mesopotamia, lived in Greensboro and raised seven children.

Cotton Ginnery, Eutaw. The cotton ginnery in Eutaw, as seen in this photo postcard, was a very busy place every fall when the crops started rolling in on overburdened wagons. In fact, it became a social center for local residents. (Lee Ann Stuckey.)

WILSON HOUSE, BUILT C. 1838. William R. Ward Jr. and his sister Mary Morgan (Ward) Glass, editor of *A Goodly Heritage: Memories of Greene County,* inherited the Wilson house in 1957. *A Goodly Heritage* was written as a cooperative effort of Greene County Historical Society members and was produced in observance of the centennial of the Civil War. (Library of Congress, Prints and Photographs Division, HABS-ALA, 32-EUTA, 12-6.)

WILLIAM RIDDLE WARD (1861–1927). The son of James Riddle Ward and Mary Caroline Morgan, William Riddle Ward Sr. married Judith Lida Meriwether (1864–1950) and had four children: Alice (b. 1888), William Riddle Ward Jr. (b. 1890), John Meriwether Ward (b. 1896), and Mary Morgan Ward (b. 1898). (W. S. Hoole Special Collections, University of Alabama.)

FOSTER MONUMENT. Frederick and Elmira Foster erected this monument in memory of their children: Frederick Ballard Foster (b. and d. 1839) and Albert Wilson Foster (1842–1843). The family lived just west of Mesopotamia Cemetery.

PALACE LIVERY STABLE. Alexander Nelson Shelton (1824–1924), the son of Leroy Shelton and Martha Isabella Lowe, was the proprietor of the Palace Livery Feed Sale Barn in the late 1800s. Alexander first married Drury Fisher, then Emma Fisher, and finally May Price. Alexander and May's four daughters—Gertrude, Ruth, Esther, and Emma—are buried in Mesopotamia Cemetery. (Lee Ann Stuckey.)

WILSON HOUSE, BUILT C. 1850. John W. Elliot worked as a watchmaker and jeweler with a shop on Prairie Street in Eutaw. After Elliot sold this house to dentist Robert E. Watkins (1829–1896), it was subsequently expanded by Robert's youngest daughter, Lucy, the wife of Edwin Wilson. The home has since been moved. (Mrs. James Edwin Banks.)

WATKINS-WILSON LOT. The Watkins-Wilson lot contains the tombstones of Dr. Robert E. Watkins; his wife, Anna Oliver (d. 1908); their daughter Lucy Bryan (Watkins) Wilson (1860–1939); and her husband, Edwin Wilson (1853–1922), an attorney from Tennessee. Dr. Watkins, a Royal Arch Mason, practiced dentistry in Eutaw.

ALEXANDER JARVIS, CONFECTIONER (1810–1869). Alexander Jarvis and his wife, Jane Grier (1817–1860), immigrated to the United States from Down County, Ireland, in 1840 and were married shortly thereafter in Boston. Alexander purchased a lot on the town square in Eutaw in the 1840s and ran a "confectionary and bakery," as well as an Irish pub. The tombstone photograph is of his granddaughter Louise Jarvis (1883–1886).

A BUSY DAY IN EUTAW, OCTOBER 14, 1893. Alexander Jarvis occupied the bottom floor of the leftmost building, with the Masonic Lodge inhabiting the top floor. Alexander was a frequent and creative advertiser in the local papers, claiming his confectionery business offered such things as "Cough Candy—a Cure Unfailing and Priceless of Worth." (W. S. Hoole Special Collections, University of Alabama.)

JARVIS ALDRIDGE (LEFT), DAVID TROTTER (CENTER), AND LOUISE JARVIS TROTTER JENKINS.
Jarvis Aldridge followed in the footsteps of his great-grandfather Alexander Jarvis and opened a variety store in Eutaw in 1933. Aldridge inherited half of the original Jarvis building after Alexander's son Franklin Pierce Jarvis died in 1914. (Obie J. Lee.)

HOME OF BECKHAM DYE PALMER, BUILT 1889. Beckham Dye Palmer Jr. (1865–1923), the son of Beckham Dye Palmer Sr. and Virginia Caroline Ward, built this home in stages between 1899 and 1909. Located on Boligee Street in Eutaw, the Palmer home was the first residence wired for electricity in Greene County. (Greene County Historical Society.)

MARIAH LOUISE (PALMER) JARVIS (1854–1933). "Panny" was the sister of Beckham Dye Palmer Jr. and the wife of Franklin Pierce Jarvis (1853–1914), both interred at Mesopotamia Cemetery. Franklin came to an untimely end when he was crushed to death in an elevator mishap at Sloss Sheffield Steel and Iron Company of Birmingham, where he had gone to announce his retirement after working 30 years. (Obie J. Lee.)

LILLIAN BARCLAY JARVIS TROTTER (1890–1975). The granddaughter of Alexander Jarvis, Lillian inherited half of the Jarvis building after his death. Shown here at age 16, she was the daughter of Franklin Pierce Jarvis and Mariah Louise Palmer. Lillian, Franklin, and Mariah are all buried in Mesopotamia Cemetery. (Obie J. Lee.)

FOSTER MARK KIRKSEY (1817–1906).
Foster Kirksey, the son of Jehu and
Nellie (Foster) Kirksey, was born in
Tuscaloosa and became a successful
planter and cotton broker, as well
as deputy sheriff (1836) and sheriff
(1845–1848) of Greene County. He
first married Jane Meriwether, and after
her death, he wed Margaretta Liston
of South Bend, Indiana. Liston was
a descendant of Revolutionary War
ensign Nathaniel Ashby of Fauquier
County, Virginia.

KIRKWOOD MANSION, KIRKWOOD DRIVE, EUTAW. Foster Mark Kirksey built the Kirkwood
Mansion, one of the most architecturally significant antebellum homes in the South. The four-story
Greek Revival mansion remained in the family for over 100 years. When Foster died, the home
passed to his son Dr. Harold Ashby Kirksey (1873–1953), a dentist, also buried in Mesopotamia.
(Al Blanton, owner of Kirkwood.)

PORTRAIT OF FOSTER MARK KIRKSEY IN PARLOR. The Kirkwood Mansion remained unfinished until after the Civil War. The lavishly furnished house was restored in the 1970s, complete with Carrara marble mantles, Waterford chandeliers, pecan groves, and eight acres of gardens. Kirksey and his second wife had nine children, two of whom died as infants. Kirksey, his second wife, sons Harold and Foster, and the two infants are all buried in Mesopotamia.

KIRKWOOD MANSION PORCH. The Kirkseys' wheelchair-bound youngest daughter, Margaretta Eliza (1879–1909), rolled to her death at the age of 29, as the upstairs balcony railings had not been installed due to the Civil War. Foster, Margaretta, and their children—Mary; Foster Jr.; Robert; Harold and his wife, Janie Coleman; Earl; and Margaretta—are all buried in Mesopotamia Cemetery. (Library of Congress, Prints and Photographs Division, HABS-ALA, 32-EUTA, 1-3.)

WILLIAM OLIVER MONROE (1835–1901). A Royal Arch Mason, William was born to John Monroe and Emily Paschal of Athens, Georgia. He married Sarah Elizabeth "Janie" DuBois, the daughter of Rev. John DuBois of Greensboro, Alabama. William's daughter J. DuBois (Monroe) Rutherford organized the first chapter of the United Daughters of the Confederacy in Greene County in 1911 and named it for him.

EUTAW WHIG AND OBSERVER. In 1846, William O. Monroe apprenticed with the *Eutaw Whig* and then purchased a half-interest in the newspaper in 1859. He bought the *Independent Observer* in 1861 and consolidated the two newspapers as the *Eutaw Whig and Observer*, which was known as one of the "most influential papers of its class in the state," per *Northern Alabama: Historical and Biographical*, published in 1888. (Alabama Department of Archives and History, Montgomery.)

SARAH ELIZABETH JANE (DUBOIS) MONROE (1839–1891). The rustic-style headstone of Janie Monroe, the wife of William O. Monroe, sits on a rock base, symbolizing that her life was built on a firm religious foundation. The scroll on her tombstone is surrounded on the right by ivy, which is associated with immortality and fidelity; on the left, the oak leaves symbolize strength, endurance, eternity, power, and longevity.

PERKINS-SPENCER HOUSE, BUILT C. 1850. William Perkins, a wealthy merchant from Kentucky, purchased six acres in 1841 on which to build his three-story Greek Revival home on Spencer Street. Listed on the National Register of Historic Places, the home is now known as the Freemount Mansion and is one of four surviving antebellum pillared mansions in Eutaw. (Library of Congress, Prints and Photographs Division, HABS-ALA, 32-EUTA, 3-1.)

WILLIAM PERKINS (C. 1808–1868). William Perkins formed a partnership with George H. Dunlap in the dry goods firm of Dunlap and Perkins of Eutaw. He and his wife, Harriet Rabb (1820–1897), and their children—Elizabeth, Harriet, William, John Rabb, Julia, and James—were all interred at Mesopotamia Cemetery.

CAPT. EDWIN REESE, CARRIAGE MANUFACTURER (B. 1812). Edwin Reese was the son of Henry Dobson Reese and Rebecca Harris of Abbeville, South Carolina. Edwin's abilities were more than likely inherited from his father, as he had been known as a mechanical genius with a remarkable talent used to construct carriages, wagons, houses, and furniture. The Reese home is featured on the cover of this book. (Carol Phillips.)

Eutaw, Ala., _____ 188

Office of Miss M. I. REESE & Co.,

----DEALERS IN----

MILLINERY, FANCY GOODS AND NOTIONS,

----CONSISTING OF----

Hats, Bonnets, Satins, Velvets, Ribbons, Silks, Flowers, &c., &c.

ALSO AGENTS FOR THE SALE OF THE "DOMESTIC SEWING MACHINE"

MISS MARY IONE REESE, MILLINERY, FANCY GOODS, AND NOTIONS. Ione (b. 1843), the daughter of Capt. Edwin Reese and Charlotte McKinstry, was the proprietor of "Miss M. I. Reese and Co.," a millinery shop in Eutaw at "the old stand, opposite the Mirror Office." She also authored several books, including *From the Cabin to the Throne.* (Carol Phillips.)

JOHN SCEARS HOME, BUILT C. 1848. Also known as Glennville, this residence was built by Jincy G. Glenn and purchased by John Scears, a planter from Springfield, in 1851. John, the son of Samuel and Martha (Chiles) Scears, married Narcissa Hoggue. Martha, John, and Narcissa are buried in Mesopotamia Cemetery. (Greene County Historical Society.)

MARTHA (CHILES) SCEARS (1786–1853). The marble tombstone of Martha Chiles, the wife of Samuel Scears (b. 1794), was carved by Alexander Herd and Brothers of Eutaw Marble Works. Martha was born in Abbeville, South Carolina, the daughter of James and Polly Chiles. Samuel Scears may be buried in Mesopotamia; if so, his tombstone is no longer standing.

RECEIPT FOR TOMBSTONE OF MARTHA SCEARS. This receipt, from the estate file of Martha Scears, indicates that her headstone and footstone cost $110 plus an additional charge for the lettering and dash. Dated August 29, 1855, it is signed by Alexander Herd and Brothers. (Greene County Courthouse, estate file of Martha Scears.)

BANKS-COLEMAN HOME, BUILT C. 1856. The Banks-Coleman home, one of four surviving antebellum pillared mansions in Eutaw, was built by George W. Shawver, proprietor of the Parapet Hotel in Eutaw. James Oliver Banks and his wife, Julia, inherited the house in 1890. It later became the headquarters for the Greene County Historical Society. (Library of Congress, Prints and Photographs Division, HABS-ALA, 32-EUTA, 8-2.)

BANKS AND COMPANY, EUTAW. Gustave Braune constructed this brick building in the 1880s. James Oliver Banks and Beckham Dye Palmer partnered in a hardware and mercantile business during the late 1880s and established Banks and Palmer, which was later reorganized as Banks and Company, specializing in building materials. (Teresa Inge Beeker.)

MARTHA JANE (COLEMAN) BANKS (1833–1868). Martha Coleman, depicted in this oil portrait, attended Mesopotamia Female Seminary, graduating in 1848; according to her certificate, she "attained such proficiency in the several branches of Science and Literature taught herein." Martha married James Oliver Banks and is buried in Grassdale Cemetery, across the street from Mesopotamia Cemetery. (Mrs. James Edwin Banks.)

WHEELER HOTEL ANNEX. The annex of the Wheeler Hotel is all that remains of the former Exchange Hotel, built on the south end of Prairie Avenue in Eutaw. In the early 1800s, Matthew Joseph Wheeler ran the hotel, which was first named Alexina House after his wife, Alexina E. Wallace. Alexina's brother John Louis Wallace operated the hotel office, and Charles B. Wallace acted as general superintendent of the railroad.

MATTHEW JOSEPH WHEELER (1835–1918). Maj. Matthew Joseph Wheeler, born in Ohio of New York parents, married Alexina E. Wallace in San Antonio, Texas, in 1867 and had six children: Alice, Charles, Edith, John Wallace, Matthew, and Alexina "Nina." The couple's youngest daughter, Nina (1886–1881), and son Wallace (1882–1945) are also buried in Mesopotamia.

ALEXINA E. WHEELER (1850–1889). The wife of Matthew Joseph Wheeler, Alexina was the daughter of Eliza Bowman and Col. James S. Wallace. She was born in Philadelphia, where her father was the chief editor of a newspaper. The Alexina House, a popular train stop near the depot, used this slogan in the 1880s: "To the Alexina House, ye hungry, thirsty and sleepy and be satisfied!"

ELIZABETH BOWMAN WALLACE. A former actress at the Louisville Opera House, Eliza married Col. James S. Wallace, an esteemed writer and editor. She moved to Eutaw and lived with her daughter Alexina and son-in-law Matthew J. Wheeler after the death of Colonel Wallace in 1865. The colonel was buried in Louisville, Kentucky.

M. JOSEPH WHEELER, WHEELER HOTEL, BEFORE 1918. Joseph Wheeler, driver, sits in front of the Wheeler Hotel in one of Greene County's first automobiles. Pictured from left to right are Martha T. Campbell, Benjamin Borden, Nina Wheeler, and possibly John Wallace Wheeler in the front passenger seat. (Fenwick Campbell Byrd.)

ALEXINA HOUSE–WHEELER HOTEL. A story in the *Tuscaloosa Times* reported the following: "Alexina house—When we strike a good thing, we can't keep it quiet, and we now feel like telling how good a thing it is to strike the Alexina House at Eutaw about breakfast, dinner, supper or bed time! Our friend, Major Wheeler, is the Prince of clever gentlemen, and a born hotel keeper; there are none who depart from his table unsatisfied, not even the most fault-finding drummer, not the overworked railroad man. Mr. John L. Wallace has charge of the office. He will be long remembered in this city as being the fortunate man in getting one of Tuscaloosa's beauties for a wife. He is courteous to all, and the 'right man in the right place.' To the Alexina House, ye hungry, thirsty and sleepy and be satisfied!" (Above, W. S. Hoole Special Collections, University of Alabama; below, Betty Banks, *Independent Observer*.)

ALEXINA HOUSE RECEIPT, 1893. John R. Hill, the son of Robert W. Hill and Elizabeth Murphy, operated the Alexina House in 1891. Hill worked as a clerk with the railroad in 1880 and then moved with his wife, Alice Caldwell Hill, and children to Birmingham, where he had taken a job as a bookkeeper by 1900. (Greene County Courthouse, estate file of W. P. Byrd.)

ROBERT W. HILL (1811–1863). Born in Georgia, Robert was the second husband of Elizabeth Epps Murphy, the daughter of William M. Murphy and Mary T. Inge. Elizabeth first married Gabriel Long Hill. Robert's tombstone is inscribed with the following Psalms verse: "Mark the perfect man and behold the upright for the end of that man is peace."

HILL LOT. Robert W. Hill; his wife, Elizabeth; daughter Sarah; sons Gabriel Long and John R.; and numerous grandchildren are buried in the Hill lot. Gabriel Long Hill was a descendant of Green Hill and Mary Long of Isle of Wight, Virginia. The family's tall marble monument was signed by carver Alexander Herd.

GREENSBORO BUGGY. The neighboring town of Greensboro, the seat of Hale County, was once a part of Greene County until Hale split off after the Civil War. Greensboro boasts 40 extant antebellum homes. Hale County was named after Stephen Fowler Hale, Greene's Civil War hero, who was interred at Mesopotamia Cemetery. (W. S. Hoole Special Collections, University of Alabama.)

Six

A CALLING CARD

The *Independent Observer* newspaper carried a column on the front page for attorneys, physicians, dentists, and other professionals to advertise their "professional cards." Many Mesopotamia notables used professional cards, including state senators and representatives. This chapter includes the Greene County professionals buried at Mesopotamia Cemetery.

The "business cards" column, also on the front page, typically contained advertisements for factors or commission merchants. The factor or commission merchant was a very significant figure in early Eutaw. Cotton factors frequently purchased goods for the plantation owners, took responsibility for transporting the goods to their clients, and advanced them money; in return, the goods were consigned to them.

A cotton farmer generally operated under a credit system by making advance arrangements with a general merchandise store. The farmer obtained merchandise from the store on credit for a year, his cotton crop acting as collateral, and settled the debt at harvest. Cotton was ginned on the plantation if the farmer was wealthy enough to afford his own equipment. The crop was then hauled by cart to a steamboat landing on the Tombigbee or Black Warrior Rivers for transport to Mobile. Prior to the railroads, Mobile was the chief cotton market and wholesale distributor in Alabama. The city boasted 22 cotton factors and 34 commission merchants in 1884–1885. It was not unusual for a commission merchant to have a home in Eutaw and an office in Mobile.

As Clement Eaton noted in *A History of the Old South*, "The factor was a versatile man of business in an agrarian society who performed many different services for the planter in addition to selling his crops. He purchased or sold slaves for his client, arranged for the hiring of slaves or the placing of the planter's children in distant schools, gave advice concerning the condition of the market or the advisability of selling or withholding his crop, and bought for his client a large proportion of the plantation supplies."

BUSINESS AND PROFESSIONAL CARDS.
This newspaper clipping, the first page of a
December 1859 edition of the *Independent
Observer*, provides an example of business and
professional cards. Commission merchants
and factors from Eutaw, Clinton, Vienna, and
Mobile advertised in this issue. Attorneys and
solicitors in chancery, primarily for Eutaw and
Greensboro, generally filled the professional
cards column. (Alabama Department of
Archives and History, Montgomery.)

SHIPPERS EXCHANGE SALOON, MOBILE. Greene County commission merchants and cotton
factors typically had offices on Commerce Street, the waterfront district in Mobile. The Shippers
Exchange Saloon, constructed at the dawn of the 20th century, is located at 51 Commerce Street.
(Library of Congress, Prints and Photographs Division, HABS-ALA, 49-MOBI, 121-3.)

THE INDEPENDENT OBSERVER. Capt. Stephen F. Nunnelee was the founder and editor of Eutaw's *Independent Observer*. Nunnelee sold the newspaper to William Oliver Monroe in 1861 to join the Confederate States Army. In 1877, he bought the *Tuscaloosa Gazette* and published it with his sons; it soon became one of the leading weeklies in the state. (Alabama Department of Archives and History, Montgomery.)

COTTON BALES, 1906. A team of oxen, hauling cotton bales from the plantation of Dr. S. M. Spencer in Knoxville, stops in the square in Eutaw prior to shipment to Mobile. Some plantations were equipped to gin and bale the cotton before shipping. (Betty Banks, *Independent Observer*.)

FINCHES FERRY LANDING, EUTAW. Finches Ferry was one of many landings along the Black Warrior River where cotton was picked up for shipment to Mobile. Others included Eutaw Landing, Three Mile Landing, Meriwether's Landing, Parhams Landing, Morrows Landing, Stave Bluff Landing, Steele's Bluff Landing, and Browns Bluff Landing. (W. S. Hoole Special Collections, University of Alabama.)

CITY OF MOBILE STEAMBOAT AT CITY WHARF, SELMA. Cotton was loaded aboard steamboats and then unloaded by draymen at the docks in Mobile. Once the crop reached the market, cotton factors arranged for the inspection of the bales and the warehousing of the cotton until transportation to its final destination. (W. S. Hoole Special Collections, University of Alabama.)

PICKENS AND GREEN RECEIPT, 1860. This receipt enumerates the cotton bales processed by Pickens and Green and shipped on the steamer *Miss Vivian*. Pickens and Green were Eutaw commission merchants with offices in Mobile. Caroline Pickens, the wife of Joseph Pickens, acted on behalf of the company since she was a widow. Duff Green, Pickens's business partner, was the husband of their daughter Rebecca. (Deborah Stone.)

FREDERICK GRIST STICKNEY, COMMISSION MERCHANT (1854–1908). Frederick Grist Stickney advertised his business as "F G Stickney, Agent" in the late 1800s, boasting the "Highest Market Price Paid for Cotton." He also promoted the sale of Gullet Gins, which were saw gins manufactured in Louisiana by Benjamin Gullet. Stickney and his wife, Mary Elizabeth Ward (1854–1896), are both buried in Mesopotamia.

JOHN BYRD, AUGUST 1907. John Byrd (center) is pictured in front of the Mobile office of commission merchants Quarles and Coleman. The son of Dr. Alexander H. Byrd and Julia W. Blocker, John married Martha Campbell, the daughter of Edward Fenwick Campbell (1827–1886) and Mary Esther Borden Cheney. (Bennett Byrd.)

GREENE COUNTY COURTHOUSE. The Greene County Courthouse was reconstructed after an 1868 fire and still appears much the same as the first building of the late 1830s. The builders were asked to use the same foundation and create something "substantially the same as the original," with a few alterations. (Greene County Historical Society.)

West Side of Square, Eutaw, Ala.

WEST SIDE OF TOWN SQUARE, EUTAW, 1890S. The west side of the square covered lots 25 to 30, first purchased by Alexander Jarvis, confectioner; Caleb W. Taylor; Charles Gates; Charles Cadle and Geary Whaley; Littleberry Pippen; and John I. Winston. The striped awning in the above photo postcard advertises "City Drug Company." (Lee Ann Stuckey.)

EMMA TOULMIN HERNDON COPP (1806–1862). Emma Sarah Toulmin, the daughter of Harry Toulmin of Mobile, married Thomas Hord Herndon, one of the earliest Greene County citizens. Herndon died in 1843 and was buried in Hale County. The Herndons' son Thomas Hord Jr. was a member of the 46th, 47th, and 48th Congress. Following the death of her first husband, Emma married John H. Copp.

ALEXANDER GRAHAM, ATTORNEY (1803–1850). Alexander Graham practiced out of the same Eutaw offices as Stephen Fowler Hale until his death in 1850. His business was advertised in February 1844 as "Graham and Hale, Attorneys and Counselors at Law and Solicitors in Chancery." Archibald Blue of Chesterfield District, South Carolina, received guardianship of Alexander and Althea's two minor daughters: Mary E. and Emma E. Graham. The marble obelisk is rich with symbolism, including a winged hourglass representing mortality ("time flies"). A passageway into the unknown or a journey to heaven is depicted by a pair of arches topped with a keystone and a banner reading "Holiness to the Lord." Alexander's tombstone is signed "A. Herd, Eutaw."

HILLIARD M. JUDGE, ATTORNEY (1819–1850). The son of James L. Judge, Hilliard established a practice with Ed de Graffenried of Eutaw and Thomas Seay of Greensboro as Seay, Judge, and de Graffenried. Hilliard served as judge of the Greene County Court in 1885 and 1886. His tall obelisk monument is signed "A. Herd, Eutaw."

SOLOMON MCALPINE, SENATOR (1800–1861). Solomon McAlpine was one of the earliest settlers in the Mesopotamia area. He married Virginia Brock, the daughter of Joseph and Helen Brock of Madison County, Virginia. Representing Greene County in the legislature from 1837 to 1840, he went on to become a state senator in 1843. Two of Solomon's brothers— Blanton of Mobile and Jefferson C. of Sumter County—served in the legislature at the same time.

SOLOMON QUINTAS MCALPINE JR. (SEATED), WITH "AUNT SUE." Solomon Quintas McAlpine (February 22, 1846–June 7, 1885) was the son of Solomon McAlpine and Virginia Brock. Solomon Quintas McAlpine Jr. (November 1, 1871–September 20, 1904) was their grandson. The family owned a large amount of land in the Eutaw area and lived just west of Mesopotamia Cemetery.

JOSEPH PICKENS MCQUEEN (1854–1904). Gen. John McQueen, commander-in-chief of the state militia of South Carolina, wed Sarah Pickens, the daughter of Col. Joseph Pickens, and the couple had son Joseph. Joseph read law with Chancellor Clark and Judge Wiley Coleman and was admitted to the bar in 1875. He married Roberta Kirksey (1856–1921), the daughter of Robert B. W. Kirksey of Marengo County, and raised seven children. (*The MacQueens of Queensdale.*)

HOME OF JUDGE MONTGOMERY, BUILT C. 1889. Lawrence H. Montgomery (1874–1956) served as tax assessor, county commissioner, and finally as probate judge of Greene County for 29 years. He was the son of Lawrence Harvey Montgomery and Annie John. Judge Montgomery first married Eula Lee Leavelle and then Virginia Davenport, both buried in Pleasant Ridge Cemetery. (Greene County Historical Society.)

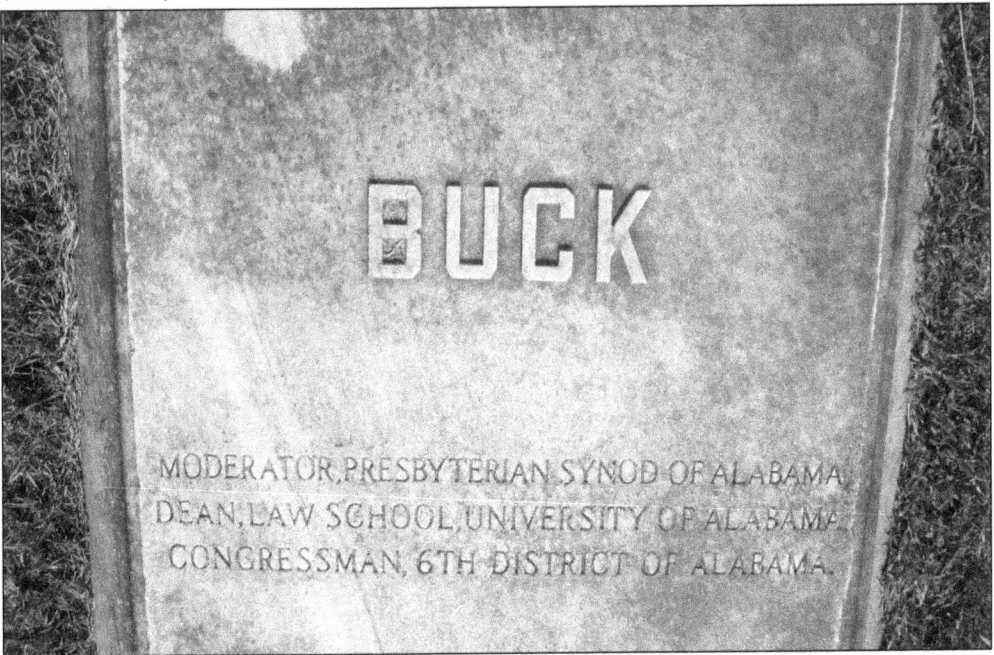

WILLIAM BACON OLIVER (1867–1948). The son of William C. and Lizzie S. (Whitehead) Oliver, William Bacon Oliver graduated from the University of Alabama in 1887 and from the law department in 1889. The inscription on his tombstone reads, "Moderator, Presbyterian Synod of Alabama; Dean, Law School, University of Alabama; Congressman, 6th District of Alabama."

WILLIAM BACON OLIVER, PUBLIC SERVANT. Oliver was appointed solicitor for the sixth judicial circuit of Alabama in 1898, a position he held until resigning in 1909. He then became dean of the law school of the University of Alabama from 1909 until 1913, when he resigned to take the position as chairman of the Democratic central committee of Tuscaloosa County. Oliver was a delegate to the Democratic National Convention in 1924 and was elected as a Democrat to the 64th and to the 10 succeeding Congresses (March 4, 1915–January 3, 1937). He served as special assistant to the attorney general at Washington, D.C., from July 22, 1939, to May 1, 1944, when he retired. He died while on a visit to New Orleans, Louisiana. (W. S. Hoole Special Collections, University of Alabama.)

PROBATE COURT ON THE SQUARE IN EUTAW. William C. Oliver (1816–1893), judge of the probate court of Greene County, was born in Nottoway County, Virginia, and died in Eutaw. His father, Isaac Oliver, and his mother, Mary A. G. Oliver, were both of English lineage. He first married Elizabeth Phillips and then Lizzie S. Whitehead. (Library of Congress, Prints and Photographs Division, HABS-ALA, 32-EUTA, 15-1.)

HOME OF JUDGE WILLIAM C. OLIVER, BUILT C. 1833. Elected probate judge in 1856, William C. Oliver served until 1868, when he was removed from office (see page 62). He was again elected probate judge in 1880, operating out of the Probate Judge's Office on the square in Eutaw. Before entering politics, Judge Oliver clerked on the steamboat *Victoria*, which ran the Warrior River between Mobile and Tuscaloosa.

AMAND P. SMITH, PROBATE JUDGE (1852–1927). Amand Pfister Smith worked as a Greene County probate judge as well as a physician. Born in Union, he practiced medicine in Knoxville for 18 years before he was appointed probate judge in 1893. Smith was a deacon in the Baptist church. (*The Book of Birmingham and Alabama.*)

AMAND P. SMITH HOME, BUILT C. 1840. Judge Smith and his wife, Mary, remodeled this home in Eutaw for their family of eight children: Amand W., Robert, Mary, Edna, Minnie, twins Sarah and Thomas, and Kirby. The Smiths added a kitchen to the rear of the house, as it had been used previously by the Eutaw Female Academy. (Library of Congress, Prints and Photographs Division, HABS-ALA, 32-EUTA, 9-2.)

HELEN (MCALPINE) TAYLOR, WIFE OF JOSEPH WALTERS TAYLOR. Helen Taylor is buried next to her father, Hon. Solomon McAlpine. Helen's husband, Joseph Walters Taylor, was born in Burksville, Cumberland County, Kentucky, in 1820 and moved to Greene County in 1838. He was elected to the senate in 1855 before becoming a newspaper editor. His tombstone is no longer standing in Mesopotamia.

WEBB LOT. The statue in the Webb lot is the largest of its kind in Mesopotamia Cemetery. The names Elmira Bell Webb (1858–1908) and Martha Young Webb (1860–1913) are inscribed on the base of the statue. Elmira and Martha were the daughters of William Peter Webb (1815–1890) and Martha Bell (1820–1875).

HOME OF WILLIAM PETER WEBB, BUILT C. 1840. A prominent Greene County lawyer, William Peter Webb was born in Lincoln County, North Carolina, the son of Judge Henry Young Webb and Francis Elizabeth (Forney) Webb. He married Martha Burwell Dabney Digges Bell, the daughter of John and Elizabeth Randolph (Bacon) Bell of Virginia. Judge Henry Y. Webb was one of five men who gathered in Cahaba in 1820 to "organize the supreme court of Alabama and hold its first term," according to descendant Lee Forney Crawford.

WEBB-ALEXANDER HOUSE, BUILT C. 1835. Dr. Henry Young Webb (1822–1893), the son of esteemed judge Henry Young Webb and Francis Elizabeth Forney, married Elizabeth Alexander in Eutaw in 1855. Elizabeth's father, Dr. Abram Alexander, gave this home to Henry and Elizabeth for their "love and affection" in 1856. It stands at 309 Main Street in Eutaw. Dr. Webb's obituary stated that he "has gone in and out of nearly every household in town as friend and physician, and he has borne with him the love, esteem and admiration of all." (Library of Congress, Prints and Photographs Division, HABS-ALA, 32-EUTA, 7-2.)

FIREPLACE IN WEBB-ALEXANDER HOUSE, C. 1935. Dr. Abram F. Alexander (1802–1866) was born in Charlotte, North Carolina, the son of Nathaniel and Jane (Harris) Alexander. Educated at Princeton, he moved to Eutaw around 1825 and practiced medicine until his death. Dr. Alexander first married Carolyn Chapman, then Kate Stokes, and finally Henrietta Adams. (Library of Congress, Prints and Photographs Division, HABS-ALA, 32-EUTA, 7-4.)

SMITH'S AMBULANCE, TOMBIGBEE RIVER. One can imagine the time it took a physician to make a house call when faced with a ferry crossing. With the Tombigbee River bordering the entire west side of Greene County and the Black Warrior River bordering the entire east side, physicians were challenged on a regular basis. (W. S. Hoole Special Collections, University of Alabama.)

DR. AUGUSTUS MEEK DUNCAN (1847–1913) AND DAVID WALTER DUNCAN (1850–1920). The Duncan brothers were interred in the only mausoleum in Mesopotamia Cemetery. Dr. Duncan, a prominent surgeon, presided over the Greene County Medical Society and served in the Confederate States Army as a corporal in Mississippi Company A, 16th Confederate Cavalry. David operated a mercantile business under the name D. W. Duncan and Company.

ANN ISABEL (DRUMMOND) LIGHTFOOT, WIFE OF DR. PHILLIP L. LIGHTFOOT. Dr. Lightfoot owned a large plantation and lived at Morven, a two-story house located south of Eutaw and named after the family plantation in Virginia. He is buried in Mesopotamia, along with his two wives: Mary Virginia Smith (1819–1855), the sister of Mrs. James Innes Thornton of Thornhill; and Ann Isabel Drummond (1827–1861). The tombstone is signed "A. Herd, Eutaw."

DR. ROBERT EMMETT WATKINS, D.D.S (1829–1896). The son of Bryan Watkins and Lucy Brown, Dr. Watkins married Anna Oliver of Nottoway County, Virginia, and had a successful dental practice in Eutaw. He and his wife are both buried in Mesopotamia Cemetery. Etched on the base of Dr. Watkins's grave is the keystone for a Royal Arch Mason.

DR. JAMES R. WARD (1824–1868). Born in North Carolina, Dr. Ward wed Mary Morgan, the daughter of Rev. Nicholas Ross Morgan. He died at the age of 44, leaving his wife with five young children: Ross, Mary, William, Genie, and Sallie. The latter two died as infants and are buried with their parents in Mesopotamia Cemetery.

Dr. Adolphus S. Murphy (1833–1907). Dr. Murphy built a home on Mesopotamia Street west of the cemetery, with doors and columns salvaged from the Mesopotamia Presbyterian Church. The Murphys owned the drug business S. S. Murphy and Company on the public square, advertising a variety of goods such as paint, medicine, and "Fancy Articles" including "pure Wines and Liquors, selected with care for Medical Purposes only."

Murphy Home, Built c. 1847. Virginia Murphy bought this home on Springfield and Pippen Streets in 1882 and lived in it with her daughter Kate, son-in-law John J. Dunlap, and granddaughter Virginia Dunlap. Dr. Murphy and Virginia Caroline Murphy (1846–1932) raised three children: Judge Samuel D. Murphy (1870–1939), James Murphy (1872–1901), and Kate Murphy Dunlap (1880–1947), all buried in Mesopotamia. (Greene County Historical Society.)

Seven

SYMBOLISM AND EPITAPHS

This chapter provides an overview of some of the symbolism and epitaphs found in Mesopotamia Cemetery that are not already presented elsewhere in the book. Tombstone symbolism is sometimes easy to interpret, such as the broken stem on a rose for a life cut short, and sometimes not so obvious. For instance, a finger pointing up is God's hand pointing to Heaven—so what does the finger pointing down represent? Surely not!

Studying the symbolism, or iconography, on a headstone, footstone, or even the lot's gate can provide clues about the deceased. What does that funny cross represent? Some crosses are heraldic and signify the eighth son. Most crosses, of course, indicate religion, and some are specific enough to denote the exact religion, which may point to a church in the area for further genealogical research.

Symbols for Masons are very common and varied, as are symbols for other fraternal organizations and memberships. The DAR (Daughters of the American Revolution) and SAR (Sons of the American Revolution) acronyms reveal that a compiled lineage back to the Revolutionary War is available for this burial.

Iconography can represent mortality, mourning, a life cut short, religious beliefs, hope, comfort, love, innocence, valor, and many other human virtues in pictorial form. One is frequently awed with the talents of the carver, as cemeteries are often abundant with museum-quality pieces. Mesopotamia is no exception—many talented carvers have contributed to this veritable outdoor museum.

The epitaphs found on tombstones in Mesopotamia typically describe where the deceased is headed, where he has been, or what tragic circumstance brought about his death. Some are simply words of comfort, such as "Gone, but not forgotten," while others express respect to the deceased with sweet clarity.

Personalized messages to the deceased that include the first name are a nice touch, whereas the description of the final "cold and silent" resting place can be a bit graphic. Since tombstone carvers typically charged by the letter, it was necessary to keep the epitaph short for those who were of modest means.

WREATH AND MOURNING DOVE. A wreath represents victory in death, while a mourning dove represents mourning; a sitting bird is thought to be guarding the soul. Daisies, often indicating a child's grave, signify the innocence of youth, and a dove, wreath, and daisies adorn the tombstone of 19-year-old Nannie Dew Taylor (d. 1909), the daughter of J. R. and M. E. Taylor.

INNOCENT LAMBS. Lambs represent innocence and often mark a child's grave. These lambs appear on the double tombstone of Emma Christine (1894–1896) and Ester Eugene Shelton (1897–1897) the daughters of Alexander N. and May Shelton. Emma's epitaph states, "Budded on earth to Bloom in Heaven," and Ester's reads, "Our darling one hath gone before to greet us on our blissful shore."

TREE STUMP AND DEAD DOVE. A tree stump indicates a life interrupted, and similarly, a dead dove represents a prematurely shortened life, while a severed tree branch suggests mortality. Annie Dura Anderson (1901–1908), the daughter of Eugene H. and Eva B. Anderson, died at the age of seven.

A BROKEN STEM. The broken stem carved on the tombstone of Hiram Colvin (1831–1887) indicates an adult's life cut short. Rosebuds—or any flower buds—symbolize a prematurely ended young life and are generally seen on the graves of infants and children. A fully bloomed rose represents an adult while also symbolizing love, beauty, and condolence.

LILY OF THE VALLEY. The Lily of the Valley symbolizes sweetness, purity, and innocence and is used as a representation of humility in religious paintings. Mary Bird (or Byrd), the daughter of Gen. Daniel Hammond Byrd and Mary E. Byrd, died on January 5, 1857, at the age of seven.

ACANTHUS AND NARCISSUS. The headstone of Eliza Aikn (Taylor) Hill (1809–1876), the wife of L. C. Hill, displays two acanthus leaves, old funerary motifs that are primarily decorative. The daffodil, however, symbolizes rebirth and resurrection, triumph of divine love and sacrifice over vanity—and according to the legend of Narcissus, selfishness and death.

FLOWERS BLOSSOMED. The partially opened rosebud on a broken stem depicted on Mollie S. Colvin's tombstone symbolizes a life cut short. Mollie (1870–1901), the daughter of Hiram and Mary Colvin, died shortly after her 21st birthday. Her epitaph completes the analogy: "Another Sweet Flower Blossom in the Dews of Heaven."

A PERSONAL TOUCH AND A ROSEBUD. Katie Louise Cunningham, the three-year-old daughter of James and C. Cunningham, died on September 15, 1872. Her tombstone is signed "A. Herd, Eutaw" and reads, "Sleep on sweet Katie and take thy rest. / God called thee home. He thought it best."

Sunflower. A sunflower adorns the mausoleum of Dr. Augustus Meeks Duncan (1847–1913) and David Walter Duncan (1850–1920), the sons of James and Elizabeth (Hitt) Duncan. The sunflower, symbolic of gratitude and affectionate remembrance, turns toward the sun, indicating brightness.

Masonic Emblem. The compass and square design on the marble monument of Duncan Dew Jr. (1832–1897) is the primary symbol of the Freemasons, the largest fraternal organization in the world. The compass and square symbolize faith and reason, and the letter G is thought to stand for God or geometry. The Masonic emblem is one of the most common symbols found on Greene County tombstones.

WEEPING WILLOW TREE. Representing perpetual mourning and grief, the willow tree is found on many early Mesopotamia tombstones. The willows are frequently accompanied with a person mourning, a column, and/or most commonly an urn. The willow and urn was one of the most popular motifs in the 18th and 19th centuries, replacing the earlier skull and crossbones or death's head funerary symbols. Malinda J. Lokey (1835–1861), the wife of Thomas B. Lokey and the daughter of Robert H. and Aselia Patterson, died at the age of 25. Her tall marble slab is signed "A. Herd," and her epitaph reads as follows: "She hath gone the bright regions of bliss to explore / Whither Jesus her Savior hath entered before / To the climes of bright glory, the city of light, / To the blessed fruition of heavenly delight."

Sheaf of Wheat, Calla Lily, and Ferns. The tombstone of John Scears, who died on February 21, 1889, at 64 years old, bears a sheaf of wheat, symbolizing a full life and generally found on the stone of a person who lives to a "ripe old age." A sheaf of wheat is also a popular Masonic symbol. The floral arrangement on the bottom of Scears's tombstone includes a calla lily, which represents marriage, fidelity, and majestic beauty, and a fern, which indicates humility, solitude, and sincerity. A floral bouquet symbolizes remembrance and the beauty and brevity of life. Scears's epitaph states, "Tis not our father who lies buried here / Tis but the Casket that did hold the gem / His Father and his God had need of him / So sent his messenger to call him Home / To give him an 'eternal rest.'"

BROKEN COLUMN. A column represents a noble life, while a broken column suggests a life cut short and possibly the loss of the family head. This epitaph reads, "In loving remembrance of / Robert Percy Hairston / Born at Eutaw, Ala. Feb. 12, 1863 / Assassinated at Haysville / Greene Co., Ala. / Dec. 21, 1892 / 'Eternal rest grant unto him, O Lord.'"

ONLY SLEEPING, CLOUDS. The marble tombstone of Johnny S. Scears (1856–1857), the son of John and Narcissa Scears, depicts a child sleeping peacefully on a bed of clouds. Clouds typically represent heaven or the divine abode, and a sleeping child evokes eternal rest. His epitaph reads, "Our Babe is in Heaven."

HAND DESCENDING FROM CLOUDS, BROKEN CHAIN. On the tombstone of Robert S. Scarbrough (1854–1889), a hand descends from the clouds clutching a link that has broken away from the rest of the chain. The hand symbolizes the hand of God taking Robert Scarbrough (the chain link) to heaven. The remaining chain links are family members who have been left behind to mourn.

PAIR OF BOOTS. The boots on the tombstone of J. R. Collins (September 3, 1888–September 4, 1890), the son of R. C. and M. L. Collins, are unusual. In this case, the symbolism is explained with the epitaph "Little Feet that never went astray."

WHERE ARE THEY GOING?
The epitaph on the tall marble slab of Artimisse Dunlap (1824–1854), the consort of R. J. Dunlap, indicates in a rather sad way where she is headed after death. Her epitaph reads as follows: "But not forever, in the silent tomb / Where thou art laid, thy kindred shall find room / A little while, a few short years of pain. / And one by one we'll come to thee again."

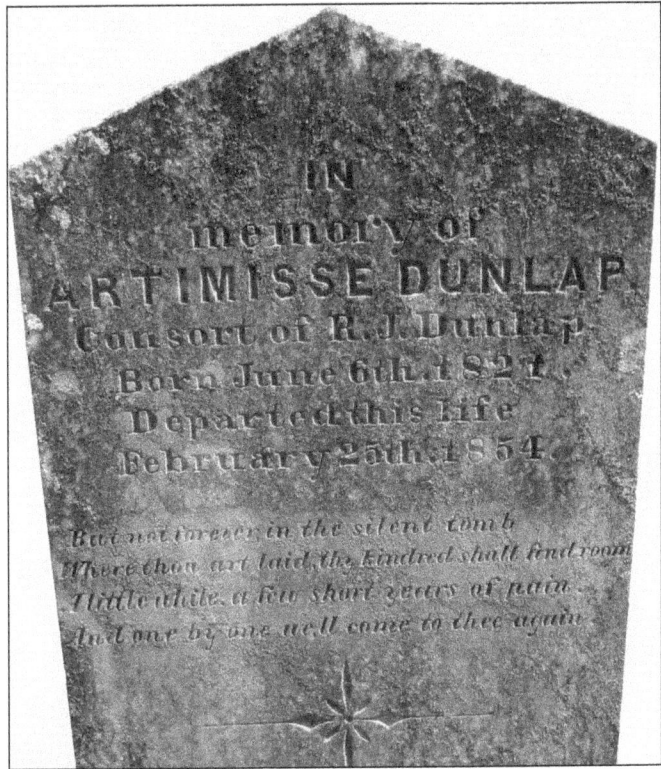

CLASPING HANDS. Alexander Falconer's marble stone bears the image of clasped hands, which represent a spouse departing. His epitaph solidifies the symbolism: "Lo where this silent marble weeps / A friend, a husband, a father sleeps, / A heart within whose sacred cell / The peaceful virtues loved to dwell. / Death to thee is bliss eternal, / Our loss is they eternal gain, / Thou dwell'st where spring is ever vernal / And life asserts its right to reign."

123

FINGER POINTING UP. A finger pointing up indicates where the soul has gone (heaven), whereas a finger directed down represents God pointing to his chosen. E. S. Morrow (1862–1897), John Poole (1875–1910), George H. Dunlap (1807–1892), and Robert W. Hill (d. 1863) share the following Psalms verse: "Mark the perfect man and behold the upright for the end of that man is peace."

HEART. The ornately carved marble slab of William R. Hamlett (c. 1801–1854) displays a heart representing bereavement, as indicated in his epitaph: "Peace to thy slumbers beloved one, / And till life's wearied course is run / Thy voice shall guide us when we pray / Teaching our bereaved hearts to say / Thy will be done."

INDEX

BIBLIOGRAPHY

AGS Field Guide No. 9: Symbolism in the Carving on Gravestones. Massachusetts: Association for Gravestone Studies, 2003.

Cormany, James R. "Gustave Braune—'At the Sign of the Big Watch,' Eutaw, Alabama." *Silver* Magazine. November-December 1994.

Crawford, Lee Forney. *William Webb Crawford: Family Sketches Genealogies.* Birmingham, AL: Roberts and Son, 1958.

DeLand, T. A., and A. Davis Smith. *Northern Alabama: Historical and Biographical.* Birmingham, AL: Smith and DeLand, 1888.

Greene County Historical Society and Mary Morgan Glass. *A Goodly Heritage: Memories of Greene County.* Clarksville, TN: Josten's, 1977.

Hennessey, Melinda Meek. "Political Terrorism in the Black Belt: The Eutaw Riot." *Alabama Review* Vol. XXXIII, No. 1 (January 1980).

Heritage Publishing Consultants and the Greene County Heritage Book Committee. *The Heritage of Greene County, Alabama.* Clanton, AL: Heritage Publishing Consultants, 2001.

http://magnolia.cyriv.com/DynamicTree/Cemetery/Search/CmDtl.asp?CID=8

Huey, Mattie McAdory. *History of the Alabama Division United Daughters of the Confederacy.* Opelika, AL: Post Publishing Company, 1937.

Keister, Douglas. *Stories in Stone.* Salt Lake City, UT: Gold Smith.

Lancaster, Clay. *Eutaw: The Builders and Architecture of an Antebellum Southern Town.* Clarksville, TN: Josten's, 1979.

MacElyea, Annabella Bunting. *The MacQueens of Queensdale: A Biography of Col. James MacQueen and His Descendants.* Charlotte, NC: 1916.

Reese, Mary E. *Genealogy of the Reese Family in Wales and America: from their arrival in America to the present time.* Richmond, VA: Whittet and Shepperson, 1903.

Remington, W. Craig and Thomas J. Kallsen. *Historical Atlas of Alabama, Volume 1, Historical Locations by County.* Tuscaloosa, AL: University of Alabama, 1999.

Rogers, William Warren Jr. *Black Belt Scalawag: Charles Hays and the Southern Republicans in the Era of Reconstruction.* Athens, GA: University of Georgia Press, 1993.

The Book of Birmingham and Alabama. Birmingham, AL: Birmingham Ledger, 1914.

The Walking and Driving Guide to Historic Eutaw, Alabama. Eutaw, AL: Greene County Historical Society.

Webb, Rev. F. B. *Centennial Sermon of Eutaw Church.* Synod of Alabama, 1924.

Visit us at
arcadiapublishing.com